SOCIAL SENSITIVITY

SUNY Series in The Philosophy of the Social Sciences
Lenore Langsdorf, EDITOR

SOCIAL SENSITIVITY

A Study of Habit and Experience

*

by
JAMES M. OSTROW

*

State University of New York Press

Published by
State University of New York Press, Albany

For information, address State University of New York
Press, State University Plaza, Albany, NY 12246

Library of Congress Cataloging-in-Publication Data

Ostrow, James M., 1956-
    Social sensitivity: a study of habit and experience / by James M. Ostrow.
        p.   cm. — (SUNY series in the philosophy of the social sciences)
        Bibliography: p.
        ISBN 0-7914-0215-0. — ISBN 0-7914-0216-9 (pbk.)
        1. Social structure. 2. Phenomenological sociology. 3. Intersubjectivity.
        I. Title. II. Series: SUNY series in philosophy of the social sciences.
    HM73.O89   1989
    302'.12—dc20   89-35027
                                                                    CIP

10 9 8 7 6 5 4 3 2 1

CONTENTS

PREFACE

This book explores the social structure of immediate experience. At the heart of my study is a theory of habitual sensitivity that has its origins in the writings of Maurice Merleau-Ponty and John Dewey. I focus particularly on how Merleau-Ponty's theory of the habitual body is better suited to a recovery of the experiential depth of social life than Alfred Schutz's theory of taken-for-granted knowledge. It is clear that Schutz's theory of habituality has had a pervasive influence on how phenomenological philosophy is understood and applied within sociology. In suggesting an alternative perspective I mean to establish different grounds for a phenomenologically informed theory of social life—one that more adequately grasps our nonreflective involvement in the social environment. Each chapter expands on the following claim: Human existence is inherently social by virtue of the sensitivity that immerses us within the world prior to the discrimination of objects of knowledge. Implications of this claim for the sociological problems of intersubjectivity, self and self-awareness, and social position are explored.

I was introduced to the phenomenological problem of habit by Victor Kestenbaum. Throughout the composition of this book he has remained an advocate and, not always painlessly, my strongest critic. He cannot be held responsible for whatever deficiencies exist in my arguments, but it is certain that he deserves the most thanks for guidance in this and most of the scholarly work that I have produced over the past twelve years. No one has had a more lasting impact on my habits of intellectual expression. I am indebted to George Psathas for teaching me the sociological arts of observation and analysis. His advice and support have been crucial in the pursuit of a sociological theory of experience. This is also the case for Kurt H. Wolff, whose concern for both logical precision and definition of theoretical vision has helped to sharpen many of my formulations.

vii

It is impossible to acknowledge everyone who has provided invaluable support for this work. Jeff Coulter helped me to develop a greater sensitivity to problems of conceptual clarity in my arguments. Erazim Kohák's writings and classes inform much of what I take to be phenomenological reflection. David Rehorick and David M. Levin made useful comments on an early draft of the manuscript. I also thank Tim Anderson for his constant support as both a close friend and colleague. Rosalie Robertson of SUNY Press provided much needed guidance throughout the publication process.

I owe much to my parents, Richard and Barbara Ostrow, for their lasting encouragement and support. If they ever had doubts about the completion of this work they never expressed them, displaying only enthusiasm for signs of progress as they appeared. Christine Miyasato-Ostrow remains my most important source of personal support and criticism. As a painstaking critic of the grammatical style and level of literary clarity of my arguments, she is the coproducer of this book, and it is to her and Emily, who kindly delayed being in the world until the first draft was complete, that I dedicate it.

Chapter One

Introduction:
The Sense and Significance of Social Life

> Consistent as well as humane thought will be aware of the hateful
> irony of a philosophy which is indifferent to the conditions that
> determine the occurrence of reason while it asserts the ultimacy
> and universality of reason.
>
> John Dewey
Experience and Nature

In an elegant rendering of Max Weber's conception of the focus
of sociology Clifford Geertz remarks that human beings are
"suspended in webs of significance that they themselves have spun"
(Geertz, 1973: 5). Disagreements continue over both what factors
take precedence in the formation and transformation of social
conditions of our existence as well as the degree of impact that
individuals may have on such processes. This book stands apart
from these disputes and confines itself to the problem of laying
conceptual grounds for explicating our "suspension" within social
environments at their first-order, nontheoretical level of *significance* in everyday life. I argue for an analysis of the structure of
immediate experience. More specifically, I try to show how the
social forces and relationships that situate human behavior and
consciousness are comprehensible in terms of what John Dewey
would call the "qualitative immediacy" or nonthematized "sense" of
the social world.

This chapter delineates the importance of a recovery of the
qualitative immediacy of social life for sociological theory. I
contend that this recovery must rest upon a theory of habit or, as it is
further elaborated, a theory of acquired *sensitivity*. The topic of
habitual sensitivity is introduced in terms of the central themes of

1

the book: Intersubjectivity, the sociality of self and self-awareness, and the dialectic between "objectively given" social position and the "personal" experience of inhabiting social settings.

Sense and signification

"The sense of a thing," Dewey writes, "is an immediate and immanent meaning; it is meaning which is itself felt and directly had" (Dewey, 1929: 261). Dewey contends that the sense of the world is the experiential foundation of its conceptual significations. Things are, for example, "poignant," "comfortable," or "fearful" not simply or primarily through conceptualization or knowledge. I may possess concepts of "poignancy," "comfort," or "fear," but the qualities of life that they signify are not constituted by, although they may be colored by the use of, these concepts. The analytical problem is, again using Dewey's terminology, to "denote" the prereflectively lived grounds for the intelligibility and use of concepts. It is only then that philosophy can discovery the "conditions that determine the occurrence of reason" (Dewey, 1929: 120), or the occurrence of the conceptual significations through which we can *know* the significance of things.

Knowledge enables us to isolate conditions, causes, and other so-called "objective" aspects of human circumstances, as well as the particular behaviors, feelings, and other apparently "subjective" features that display themselves. Yet at the level of sense—of having the world in its qualitative immediacy—the various discernible "objective" and "subjective" components of circumstances are not distinguished as such. We could say, for instance, that one feels fear "toward," responds with fear "because of," or finds that a stranger walking by at night "looks" frightening. We thereby use conceptions of fear to know the meaning of a particular event. Yet these are examples of meaning at the level of signification, not sense. At the level of sense the stranger is not conceived of as frightening; he *is* frightening—that is just what his presence is, irreducibly, at this fearful moment. Prior to reflection my response and his presence are a single phenomenon; they are interwoven through what Merleau-Ponty calls a "cohesion without concept" (Merleau-Ponty, 1968: 152). It is true that this cohesiveness is discernible only through conceptual distinctions. We must not, however, forget the qualitative whole that antecedes these distinctions. As Dewey says, "to be a composite is one thing; to be capable of reduction to a composite by certain measures, is another thing" (Dewey, 1929: 143). The sense of the world is "just what it is as it exists," not so many "effects" or "signs" of something else (Dewey, 1929: 96).

In their immediate and immanent sense things and circumstances are significant with a force that often leads us to use the term "experience," in contrast to terms such as "action," "behavior," or "thought," to describe our contact with them. The term denotes that we not only orient to the environment through conduct and consciousness; we also undergo it and are taken or repelled by it with varying degrees of intensity. The qualities of things are at once qualities of our involvements with them, which is to say, it is through experience that the material world *matters* personally. With the concept of experience we affirm that we are under unceasing pressure to act and think in terms of a world that *matters* from the standpoint of our immersion within its qualitative immediacy.

The following chapters explore aspects of the fundamentally social character of this world. This is not to assert the primacy of "mind" over "matter," or the idea that social meaning is a "subjective construction" rather than an "objective fact." My intention is to explicate the qualitative structure of the social world, which is no less "material" than any scientifically discovered properties of the objects and processes within the physical environment. Dewey writes:

> things are poignant, tragic, beautiful, humorous, settled, disturbed, comfortable, annoying, barren, harsh, consoling, splended, fearful; are such immediately and in their own behalf . . . . These traits stand in themselves on precisely the same level as colors, sounds, qualities of contact, taste, and smell. Any criterion that finds the latter to be ultimate and "hard" data will, impartially applied, come to the same conclusion about the former. (Dewey, 1929: 96)

The "impartiality" that Dewey proposes requires nothing less than an escape from the division between "subjective" and "objective" orders of existence that has dominated Western philosophy and science since the time of Galileo. This division is founded upon what Husserl calls the "mathematization of nature" through which objects of science were separated from their experiential qualities (Husserl, 1970). The "extrusion" of immediate qualities from scientific objects left these qualities to "[hang] loose from the 'real' object" (Dewey, 1929: 265). Since the existence of experiential qualities "could not be denied they were gathered into a psychic realm of being, set over against the objects of physics" (Dewey, 1929: 265).

The premise of a dualism between "psychic" and "material" realms of existence underlies the reduction of philosophical thought to the alternative between "empiricism" and "idealism," or between treating ideas as derivations of matter or matter as derivations of ideas (Kohák, 1978: 170). Dewey and Husserl argue for a rejection of the metaphysical premise from which "all the problems regarding the relation of mind and matter, the psychic and the bodily, necessarily follow" (Dewey, 1929: 264-265). By rejecting this premise, immediate qualities are restored "to their rightful position as qualities of inclusive situations" (Dewey, 1929: 265). They are seen as neither "subjective" or "objective," but anterior to such a distinction, which is precisely Husserl's contention when he attacks the "surreptitious substitution of the mathematically substructed world of idealities for the only real world, the one that is actually given through perception, that is ever experienced and experienceable—our everyday life-world" (Husserl, 1970: 48-49).

An acceptance of the philosophical split between mind and matter has constrained theoretical possibilities within the discipline of sociology. Consequently, a theoretical focus on the immediately and immanently felt meaning of social life has been absent. I contend that this oversight is as true of the "interpretive," or "phenomenological," sociological traditions as the "explanatory," or "positivistic," traditions.

Comte introduced the discipline of sociology as an objective science of the social world. That is, social existence is subject to the same principles of demonstration and analysis that operate within the physical sciences (Comte, 1974). Durkheim expanded Comte's conception of sociology, arguing that human consciousness and action are determined causally by extrapersonal social forces and processes that can be located and tested with the same "objective" scrutiny as the data of the physical sciences (Durkheim, 1938).

With the relegation of experiential qualities to a "subjective" versus "objective" realm by the physical sciences it is not surprising that the sociological tradition of explanatory-causal analysis conceived by Comte and refined by Durkheim will not seriously entertain the idea of nonreflective sense as an analytical starting point. If experiential qualities are, so to speak, submerged inside the psyche rather than revealed outside in the material environment, then by claiming their foundational importance the observable dynamics of the social environment are treated as derivative. Their meaning and significance are taken to be determined by more primary mental processes. Hence, the return to experience is tantamount to "solipsism" with its premise of a solitary ego standing apart from and "constituting" the meanings of the world. On the other hand, if qualities of experience are "internal" rather than "external," then their disclosure is essentially a private and speculative affair. It follows that the possibility of generating publicly verifiable claims is abandoned, one's discoveries being based less on empirical evidence than on nondemonstrable intuitions about the "inner" content of mental states.

From the above perspective a focus on prereflective sense entails solipsistic theorizing and psychologistic speculation, meaning that it will at best muddle and at worst betray the central sociological objective of revealing the inherently social structure of human existence in a scientifically acceptable manner. Yet although the problem of experience appears to be obviated by the aims of the physical sciences, it is not disregarded so easily by the social sciences. Dilthey and Weber both recognized that by making human existence its object of investigation, sociology has to concern itself with the nonscientific standpoints of individuals. It is from these standpoints that the social world is originally meaningful.[1]

Weber in particular wanted to show that there is no contradiction between recognizing the importance of the "subject's standpoint" while also asserting the primacy of social determinants of human existence. His solution was to develop Dilthey's distinction between a "subjective understanding" of others *(Verstehen)* and "explanation."[2] Before aspects of human existence can be explained in terms of their social conditions they must be understood at the level of their "subjective meaning"—in terms of their interpretation by subjects who live within them. Weber argues that in the absence of such understanding sociology fails to achieve "adequacy at the level of meaning"; it fails to grasp human reality as it exists for the individuals who inhabit it.[3]

Weber's theory of *Verstehen* did more than legitimate a sociological focus on the subject's point of view. Weber established this focus as an absolute prerequisite for the articulation of social structure. Various aspects of his methodological argument have received sharp criticism—particularly his notions of the possibility of achieving "value-free" understanding of others and also of a progression from subjective understanding to causal analysis.[4] Nevertheless, the principle of *Verstehen* has endured within contemporary sociology as the solution to dealing with the inherent disparity between the standpoints of the subject and the sociologist.

Indeed, what sociologists view generally as a phenomenological approach to the analysis of social life is based upon Alfred Schutz's Husserlian reformulation of Weber's theory of *Verstehen*. As Schutz conceives it, the aim of phenomenological sociology is to develop "second-order constructs" of the "first-order constructs" that social actors employ to interpret their environments (Schutz, 1970). Schutz's distinction between first- and second-order constructs of interpretation is not merely a restatement of Weber's distinction between the values and interests of the sociologist and those of the social actor. Schutz means to distinguish practical from theoretical modes of interpretation, arguing that they involve fundamentally different ways of relating to the environment. At the same time that I theorize I also orient to my pen, this room, the passing of time, as well as the pressure of various social commitments that compel me to do this work. Many of my orientations involve interpretations that are practical, not theoretical, but they are necessary conditions for a sensible world in which theorizing is possible. These practical interpretations are of a phenomenological order different from that of theoretical interpretations. They are not operative as ideas or explicit knowledge, but are instead what

Schutz calls "typifications" or "taken-for-granted knowledge."

With Schutz's distinction between "practical" and "theoretical" interpretation *Verstehen* becomes more than a matter of transcending one's biases as a sociologist in order to view the social world more purely or "adequately." It is now the effort to grasp how individuals' typical ways of interpreting the world structure their practical involvements within it. Schutz's expansion of the problem of *Verstehen* has had considerable influence in contemporary sociology, providing, for instance, the point of departure for Berger and Luckmann's formulation of the "social construction of reality" and Garfinkel's theory of "members' methods of 'practical reasoning.' "[5]

Weber's formulation of *Verstehen*, as well as its phenomenological elaborations within contemporary sociology, have directed the attention of sociological theory to the subject's "lived" standpoint. Nevertheless, I suggest that interpretive-phenomenological sociology has retained precisely the same premise of a division between "mind" and "matter" that underlies the objectivism that is rejected by the philosophy of *Verstehen*. Person and world are presupposed to be originally separate entities that are joined through the person's interpretations. Using Dewey's terminology, interpretive sociology has generally conceived of qualities of the social world as "effects" or "signs" of the rules, concepts, knowledge, or typifications that enable the subject to interpret the world. Social life has been analyzed in terms of its *significations*, but not its *sense*. The consequence is the same as that of the presupposition of a causal relationship between social forces and personal existence. In either case the subject's direct and pervasive immersion within the social world is circumvented, and the immanent sociality of human experience remains unexplored.

An argument might be made that it was precisely Schutz's intention to make sociology attentive to the sense of the world prior to reflection. In fact, his social theory of knowledge is based upon the idea that the "givenness" of the world nonreflectively is a consequence of a subject taking for granted, or typifying, the interpretations that "bestow" meaning upon it. Schutz follows Husserl's distinction between the "transcendental" and "mundane," or "common sense," standpoints. What Schutz calls "taken-for-granted knowledge," Husserl calls the "presuppositions" of common sense that must be suspended in order to reach the transcendental sphere of "pure meaning-constitution." Schutz argues that by examining, rather than suspending, the presuppositions of common sense, we uncover the habitual constitution of prereflective reality (Schutz, 1967).

In the next chapter I discuss and criticize Schutz's theory of the habituality of common sense. Here it may be noted that by positing a "latent" form of interpretation at the heart of experience, Schutz commits the very error that he warns against: He projects the logic of "second-order constructs" onto the "first-order" sensibility of the social world. That is to say, he confuses "sense" and "signification," failing to see that the immanent sense of the world is realized in ways that must be grasped in terms of our prereflective immersion within the world—an immersion preceding processes of signification, rather than being contingent upon them.

Schutz's confusion may be attributed to his adherence to Husserl's notion of a transcendental sphere within which the world becomes meaningful through an "intentional relation" between subject and object. Merleau-Ponty argues that Husserl abandons the idea of a transcendental differentiation between subject and world in his later writings, where the "life-world" becomes increasingly the central concept of his investigations. As Merleau-Ponty reads Husserl, the "pregivenness" of the life-world is now conceived as an "operative intentionality" that is a precondition for the conscious, or "thetic," intentionality through which the world is objectified and distinguished from "oneself" (Merleau-Ponty, 1962: xviii). Whether Husserl rejects the principle of the "transcendental ego" in favor of the life-world, or retains that principle as the fundamental premise of any phenomenological investigation, is open to debate. The relevant point here is that the transcendental ego is presupposed by Schutz's formulation of taken-for-granted knowledge, or what he also refers to as habitual "schemes of interpretation" that underlie the lived meanings of social life. Schutz's conception of phenomenological sociology embodies precisely the incipient dualism between subject and world that has prevented the development of a sociological theory of prereflective experience.

The alternative phenomenological approach to social theory that I propose does not deny the existence of processes of consciousness that "make sense" of the environment, nor of sociohistorical conditions of the possibilities of sense. The problem is that these processes and conditions have been viewed traditionally as either subjective or objective, meaning they have not been grasped in the context of their experiential immanence, where a split between subject and world has not yet occurred. We may distinguish various influences on the genesis of social events and circumstances. Yet if we want to formulate the significance of these influences in human life, it is necessary to ground their force within a world whose sense is a *precondition*, as opposed to a consequence, of the intelligibility of such distinctions. In other words, we must conceptualize the sociality of human existence in terms of the "cohesion without concept" through which the social world is had as a lived reality, rather than as a composite of either tacit or explicit knowledge.

Prereflective habit

In rejecting the reduction of the pretheoretical sensibility of the social world to "typified" knowledge I do not mean to embrace what Pierre Bourdieu calls the "occasionalist illusion" of various forms of "microsociology" that view perception, feeling, conduct, and thought as though they are solely achievements of the moment (Bourdieu, 1977: 81-82). The lived sense of the world is absorbed, necessarily, within the intensity of the moment, but from an analytical standpoint we must recognize that it is also *generated* from a background of past experience. If the qualities of experience were strictly properties of the moment, there would be no context in which the sense of things and events could endure from one instant to the next. There would not exist, as Mallin puts it, an "original preparedness" that "makes it possible for the situation to disturb the subject, count for him, or motivate his articulations of it" (Mallin, 1979: 13).

We cannot recover the sociality of existence at the level that situations matter within experience if we do not also elucidate the historicity of experience. This elucidation is not accomplished, however, by locating either "internalized" norms, schemes, and typifications, or "external" determinants. An individual's or culture's past does not simply lie behind present experience, as if the past were reducible to a constellation of latent information or causal factors. Indeed, when we return our analytical focus to the qualitative immediacy of experience, we discover its inherently historical structure, thereby discovering phenomenological grounds for its socially conditioned character.

Victor Kestenbaum reveals that an interesting similarity between the philosophies of Dewey and Merleau-Ponty is their similar use of the concept of habit to demonstrate that the past is integral to the texture of the present (Kestenbaum, 1977). Neither Dewey nor Merleau-Ponty mean to equate the phenomenon of habit with the sort of tacitly operative knowledge of the environment that is posited by Schutz. As a person's fundamental, nonreflective familiarity with the world, habit is a precondition for the intentional determination of distinct objects of knowledge.

Dewey and Merleau-Ponty also oppose the behavioristic reduction of the meaning of the term "habit" to acquired neurological "reflexes" or autonomic tendencies to repeat behaviors. In their writings habits are neither programed "responses" nor routinized behaviors: Habit is the embodied *sensitivity* to a sensible world, and in this respect it provides for a field of behavioral possibilities in experience. There is a precedent for such a notion of habit in ordinary language where, as Brett notes,

> The category of habitual activity is almost certainly comprised of a continuum of cases ranging from those which involve blind and stereotyped responses to nearly identical situations to those in which attentiveness and variation are an essential part. (Brett, 1981: 369)

Dewey and Merleau-Ponty may be seen to be developing the implications of the latter meaning of habituality for understanding the foundations of sense in prereflective experience.

It is clear, however, that, the versatility of ordinary language notwithstanding, behavioristic conceptions of habit predominate within contemporary philosophical and social scientific discourse. Charles Camic argues that the absence of the concept of habit from sociological analyses is owed largely to the efforts of sociologists to differentiate their enterprise from that of psychology, where behaviorism has clearly controlled the discourse on habit (Camic, 1986).[6] The monopoly that behaviorism has exercised over the definition and study of habit also contributes to what Kestenbaum shows to be the failure of both critics and admirers of Dewey and Merleau-Ponty to understand the role of the habitual in their respective philosophies (Kestenbaum, 1977).

In later chapters I will explore sociological implications of the theory of habituality upon which Dewey and Merleau-Ponty developed their philosophies of experience. Yet in order to escape the linguistically based misunderstanding that has befallen both writers I have chosen "sensitivity" rather than "habit" as the central term of these explorations. I do this not as an abandonment of the concept of habit, but, on the contrary, as a way of emphasizing its centrality within a phenomenological philosophy of experience.

The term "sensitivity" also has various meanings within ordinary and theoretical discourse, ranging from a strictly physiological reference to the sensory responsiveness to stimuli to a purely psychological reference to emotional susceptibility. Between these extremes our language recognizes the habitual entanglement of sensibility and sensory perception. A painter may be sensitive to the subtleties of line, an investor to the mood of the market, a physician to a patient's despair or hope, or a lover to the other's "change of heart." Sensitivity provides at once a "feel for," as well as a predisposition to undergo, particular qualities of existence. It is the embodied medium for the "presence of the past" (Webb, 1976) within experience. Through sensitivity we are immersed within situations that are meaningful before we reflect on "what they mean," or, in Dewey's terms, situations that have sense prior to their signification.

Intersubjectivity as a problem of habit

The theories of habit developed by Dewey and Merleau-Ponty are the point of departure for my contention that our sensitivity to the existence of other persons is a fundamental part of the immanent sense of the world. I develop a theory of intersubjectivity, arguing that it must be grasped in terms of the habitual texture of prereflective experience. Schutz also develops a theory of inter-subjectivity that is, in turn, based upon his conception of habit-uality. I reject Schutz's formulation of intersubjectivity on the same grounds that I oppose his reduction of habit to "taken-for-granted knowledge": In either case, Schutz projects the logic of reflection onto the structure of immediate experience. By proposing alternative notions of habit and intersubjectivity, I hope to provide a theoretical foundation for explorations of the qualitative immediacy of social life.

When Schutz argues that intersubjectivity is a matter of taken-for-granted knowledge, he means to contest Husserl's belief that our ability to directly perceive other persons as subjects of their own experience is intrinsic to the structure of consciousness. Husserl claims that intersubjective perception is a transcendentally given capacity discovered within the "presuppositionless" sphere of phenomenological reflection. Schutz contends that the logic of Husserl's own formulation of the *problem* of intersubjectivity demonstrates the futility of attempting such a discovery. Husserl poses the problem as follows: How can we perceive others as conscious subjects when, by the very act of perception, their bodies become *objects* of *our* consciousness (Husserl, 1960)? For Schutz, the solution lies within the habitual composition of the "common-sense sphere": We typify the interpretations that are required to perceive the other's body as a "sign-signitive system" representative of his or her underlying experience (Schutz, 1967).

I reject the assumption that our ability to perceive the other's body as a locus of experience is fundamentally a problem of *consciousness*. Whether that assumption leads to positing an essential process of intentionality or to designating "sedimented" schemes of interpretation as the basis of intersubjectivity, it harbors the theoretical prejudice of a dualism between mind and matter. More specifically, it presupposes the objectification of the human body, relegating it to the realm of "matter."

Merleau-Ponty demonstrates that the perception of others' bodies as the expressions of their thoughts and feelings is no more a problem of consciousness than having one's own body as *lived* prior to its being posited as an object. I follow Merleau-Ponty in arguing that the body is not in the first place an object of consciousness; it is the preobjective medium of consciousness. Experience is necessarily corporeal, and it is in terms of our corporeal inherence in the world that we perceive the other's body directly as an experiencing person (Merleau-Ponty, 1962).

With Merleau-Ponty's theory of the lived body the problem of intersubjectivity shifts from one of consciousness to one of sense: How does social copresence structure the qualitative immediacy of situations? At the level of sense other persons and their conduct are never reducible to signs or, speaking hermeneutically, a "text" that I interpret in either a reflective or taken-for-granted manner. When I perceive others, I also undergo their presence; I inhabit a situation qualified by our copresence. We are, to use a term from Gestalt psychology, in *contact* (Perls, Hefferline, and Goodman, 1951) through Merleau-Ponty's "cohesion without concept." It is within such contact that our *visibility* to one another is comprised of more than the contents of our consciousness. It is a lived foundation of consciousness, or a basic structure of the immanent sense of the world.

If the corporeality of experience provides for our essential capacity to directly perceive and express ourselves to other persons, that capacity is fulfilled through our *sensitivity* to the visibility of our lived bodies within a shared world. This sensitivity is the preobjective medium of our communication with one another; it is the intersubjective context within which our social relations *matter* in experience. Intersubjectivity is now understood as a problem of habit, but not out of consolation for its lack of transcendental status. Habit is conceived here not as taken-for-granted knowledge or schemes of interpretation, but as the preobjective "preparedness" for situations that are thereby available for "interpretation." Intersubjectivity is an essential mode of our habitual preparedness for the immediately and immanently felt sense of situations.

Solipsism is, in the final analysis, rendered implausible only by locating the sociality of human existence at precisely that point where solipsism can stake its claim: The point at which the world is *personally* significant in its immanence.[7] The existence of others is intrinsic to my own existence because, prior to any conceptual distinction between myself and the world or, therefore, between myself and others, I am habitually sensitive to situations that are qualified by our copresence. The world of my experience is socially significant before I turn toward others "thetically" or "interpretively" and before I affirm or negate their expressions as significations of otherwise unrevealed contents of the mind.

Self-awareness prior to self-objectification

The idea that there is a habitual, preobjective significance to the presence of others in my experience suggests the development of an alternative to the predominant sociological approach to the topic of "self." At issue is not the traditional assertion that the self is an inherently social phenomenon, but rather the level at which its sociality has been conceived. Regarding its level of conceptualization, the self may be viewed as a casualty of the bifurcation of subject and world: it has been theoretically uprooted from the sense of the world in experience. A theory of intersubjective sensitivity helps us to recover the social contact that antecedes the disengagement of person from environment by reflection, thus helping to provide grounds for the delineation of a self that is intact within its original social medium.

The conception of self that has become virtually standard within sociology is developed systematically be George H. Mead in his elaborations of Charles H. Cooley's concept of the "looking-glass self." According to Mead, the self is constituted through an interactional process of reflexive "objectification" through which we take the attitude of others toward ourselves as objects of interpretation and judgment. Mead asserts that in the absence of reflexive consciousness—of recognizing our manner and appearance as objects of others' awareness—there exists no self. Through such consciousness we "appear as selves in our conduct" (Mead, 1932: 185), meaning that we develop the "roles" within which we think and behave in response to the expectations of others.

Hence, the self is claimed to be constituted essentially by our taking others' verbal and nonverbal gestures to be *significations* of what we are. Yet this formulation of the logic of self-awareness begs the question of self; it does not account for why the "object" of reflexive awareness should be taken to be "oneself." As soon as the intersubjective dimension of experience is recognized, self-awareness can no longer be reduced to the positing of objects of consciousness. In fact, the very topic of self-awareness draws reflection into the sphere of intersubjective sense. I experience others' responses to me in terms of the *situations* that we are steeped within prior to any posited separation between myself and the world. The problem is to disclose the *preobjective* sensitivity to one's corporeal forcefulness within others' experiences.

The work of Erving Goffman provides a point of departure for this disclosure. Goffman adheres to Mead's principle of "self-objectification" throughout his writings.[8] He sometimes alludes, however, to the need to go beyond this principle when elucidating the sociality of self. Hence, on the one hand, Goffman contends that behavior in social settings is largely mediated by our orientation to others' exhibited impressions of ourselves. On the other hand, Goffman has warned on occasion that much of what he claims about the process of "impression management" is metaphorical. He notes that if we do constantly monitor others' expressions self-reflexively, we are often "scarcely aware" of doing so (Goffman, 1959: 75). In acknowledging this I believe that Goffman refers implicitly to the limitations of his own analytical attributions of meaning to the events he describes. I hope to reveal the nature of this limitation, as well as that of the predominant sociological theory of self upon which Goffman's framework is based.

An analysis of Goffman's work is particularly suitable for the present discussion, since the inadequacy of his theoretical perspective lies precisely in its failure to address the ways that his own descriptions catch the prereflective intensity of the present. I essentially posit the plausibility of one of Goffman's examples within an analytical framework other than his own, thereby specifying the dimension of the social dynamics of experience that is obscured by his own formulations of what we mean to accomplish in the company of others. Goffman's descriptions lend themselves to such reanalysis because they manifest a constant emphasis on the primacy of the social situation for what persons do, perceive, and literally are as individuals. That is exactly what I want to emphasize; however, I seek to explicate the social situation as an unreflected medium of experience. Apart from his theoretical standpoint, Goffman's descriptions reveal the prereflective conditions of self-awareness. More specifically, the sensitivity to our corporeal impact within the situations that we share with others is an intersubjective precondition for "reading" others' verbal and nonverbal conduct as indications of "ourselves."

The subject as a meeting of two pasts

Mead claims that a sense of self formed in response to "significant others" is a developmental prerequisite for a self formed in response to the "generalized other"—defined as the general rights and expectations of the "group" or "society" (Mead, 1932). The idea that knowing the expectations of specific persons is developmentally prior to knowing the expectations of a "group" can hardly be disputed. Yet we must add that every "significant other" is also a "generalized other" in the sense that the other person is no more reducible to determinant, objective characteristics than I am. We perceive and express ourselves to one another in the context of the "generalized," preobjective texture of our shared situation. This is as true of the direct encounter between mother and child as it is of the more elliptical encounter between a "player" and his "team" as a whole. Our awareness of one another and of ourselves is in either case bound to an environment that is already "there" before our separate consciousnesses ever begin constituting its particular meanings.

Yet situations are not merely *preconstituted* environments, as if persons were nothing more than "froth on the deep stream of matter" (Luckmann, 1983b: 67)—mere appendages to the history of the world. It is better to say that our situations are *instituted* (Merleau-Ponty, 1970) by our sensitivity to the possibilities of experience that environments "pose" for us without reflection. This sensitivity is neither a latent content of the "mind" nor a mere physical response to "internal stimuli." It is the embodied habituality of *sense*—the historicity of the preobjective entanglement of subject and environment.

One version of an attempt to unravel the interwovenness of the personal history of individuals and the "objective" history of the settings that they inhabit is provided in the work of Pierre Bourdieu. Bourdieu uses the concept of "habitus" to conceive of the relation between person and environment as a prepersonal, historically emergent structure, although one that is comprehended adequately only in terms of the habituality of everyday life. Sociohistorical forces are operative for individuals not as known phenomena, but through the embodied dispositions of "practical sense." These dispositions comprise the common habitus of a group, class, or culture, which provides for our shared inherence within a familiar, "only natural" world. Habitus is, according to Bourdieu, the sociohistorically embodied "sense of reality":

> The objective structures which science apprehends in the form of statistical regularities (e.g., employment rates, income curves, probabilities of access to secondary education, frequency of holidays, etc.) inculcate through the direct or indirect but always convergent experiences which give a social environment its *physiognomy*, with its "closed doors," "dead ends," and limited "prospects," that "art of assessing likelihoods," as Leibniz puts it, of anticipating the objective future, in short, the sense of reality or realities which is perhaps the best-concealed principle of their efficacy. (Bourdieu, 1977: 85-86)

Bourdieu is elaborating on Marx's idea that the "objective forces" of human life function most pervasively at the level where, from the standpoint of individuals, they are least visible. Habitus is "history turned into nature" (Bourdieu, 1977: 78), that is, "second nature": Not being candidates for attention, the conditions of inhabiting the environment are seen, and seen historically, only in reflection. In practice—on the plane of their functioning—they are taken absolutely, without contemplation, as the "natural order of things." Hence, the self-evidence of the world, or what Husserl calls the "fact world," taken "just as it gives itself" (Husserl, 1931: 96), is predicated on the habitual attachment to an historically specific context of limits and options.

What is absent from Bourdieu's analyses are descriptions of habitus at the level of preobjective sensitivity. As a matter of fact, he claims at various points throughout his writings that the phenomenological problem of immediate experience is superfluous sociologically, inasmuch as habitus originates outside of and prior to individual experience. I will argue that Bourdieu fails to recognize the phenomenological implications of his own definition of habitus as a "system of durable, transposable dispositions" (Bourdieu, 1977: 72). He successfully avoids the reification of habituality into a repeated gesture, routinized behavior, or static content of the mind. Embodied disposition is, as Dewey says, "projective" (Dewey, 1929), or in Bourdieu's terms, a "generative principle of regulated improvisations" (Bourdieu, 1977: 78). Nevertheless, by ignoring prereflective experience, Bourdieu misses the chance to ground habitus in the immanent sense of the world.

Utilizing the environment of the elementary school classroom, I will focus on the pupil's experience in order to explicate habitus as embodied sensitivity. Bourdieu provides a precedent for this focus in his own study of the reproduction of class structure by the educational system. Here he insists against the idea that class reproduction through schooling is reducible to the system's mirroring of already existing social relations. Bourdieu argues that social inequality is legitimized tacitly through the "relatively autonomous" workings of pedagogic environments (Bourdieu and Passeron, 1977). Yet in the absence of an inquiry into dynamics of immediate experience, Bourdieu does not locate the workings of the school within the habituality of the pupil's world—the very world within which the institution has its pervasive, habitual force.

I will analyze one example of pupils' participation within a math lesson in a public elementary school classroom. The theories of intersubjectivity and self-reflexivity developed up to that point are applied to a conceptualization of pupils' embeddedness within the institutional context of classroom life. I hope to demonstrate that intersubjective sensitivity is the medium through which habitus has its original significance within experience.

When the power of the past is disclosed at the level of experience that precedes the separation between person and world in reflection, the dualism between "subjective" and "objective," or what Marx calls "material," history collapses as well. The genesis of the personal significance of the world—of the ways that situations can have sense at the moment and retain their sense over time—is as much an expression of the past experience of the individual as it is of the sociohistorical forces that shape the environmental circumstances of experience. Our sensitivity is the preobjective nexus of these two pasts; it is only in terms of this sensitivity that they can be grasped in their immanence, as the singularly historical texture of experience.

Social sensitivity

Dewey contends that "having meaning is a prerequisite for knowing" (Dewey, 1925: 18-19). Sociological theory has for the most part ignored this prerequisite; the consequence is a failure to elucidate the fundamental sociality of human existence. When we turn our attention to immediate experience, we discover that it is pervasively social by virtue of the very sensitivity that steeps us within the world before it ever becomes an object of reflection. At this level of involvement within the world—this "cohesion without concept"—I find myself "inextricably interwoven" (Merleau-Ponty, 1962: 381) with, and feel my own corporeal forcefulness within, the situations of others. I do not "constitute" this interwovenness with others; it is the medium for, rather than an object of, consciousness, and this medium is historical—a "meeting of two pasts" (Bourdieu, 1984: 315). Sensitivity is my preparedness for a social world and in this way establishes the very foundation for knowing its significance. We must explore the experiential preconditions of such knowledge, thus avoiding the "hateful irony" of a philosophy that fails to do so.

Chapter Two

From Taken-For-Grantedness to Sensitivity: Toward a Social Theory of Immediate Experience

All of the past one finds useful is "usable" because it is of the present and because both present and past are essentially irrelevant to the whole manner of "use."

James Agee
Let Us Now Praise Famous Men

Every present as it arises is driven into time like a wedge and stakes its claim to eternity.

Maurice Merleau-Ponty
Phenomenology of Perception

In the preface to the *Phenomenology of Perception* Merleau-Ponty expresses wonder at the "miracle of related experiences" (Merleau-Ponty, 1962: xx). The general effort of social theory to explicate the social foundations and character of human consciousness and behavior turns on the phenomenological problem of "related experiences"—the problem of how past experience provides a background of sense for the present. The sociohistorical forces and interpersonal relationships that condition and determine a person's values, beliefs, ideas—his very "selfhood"—do so only by virtue of the "presence of the past" (Webb, 1976) within immediate experience.

Owing largely to the influence of Schutz, social theory has recognized the importance of explicating the "sedimentations" of past experience within the present. In fact, the Weberian problem of *Verstehen* is often, thanks to Schutz, reformulated as an issue of explicating the forms of knowledge that are sedimented at the "practical" level of social life. It is perhaps true that most of what has come to be known as "phenomenological" within sociology takes its

21

departure from Schutz's theory of "taken-for-granted" knowledge. This theory has contributed substantially to a reorientation of the sociological focus on human beliefs and consciousness from "ideas," as Berger and Luckmann put it, to "common-sense knowledge" or "what people 'know' as 'reality' in their everyday non- or pretheoretical lives" (Berger and Luckmann, 1966: 5).[1]

Although Schutz recognizes the prereflective status of a person's everyday understanding of the world, I believe his formulations prove insufficient for explicating the prereflective experience of social life. By contrast, the writings of both Maurice Merleau-Ponty and John Dewey provide a firm basis for doing so. Schutz recognizes the difference between the experientially "lived" (which he discusses in terms of what Husserl calls the "internal-time consciousness") as opposed to the "reflected." However, unlike Merleau-Ponty or Dewey he does not see that the theoretical distinction between "lived" and "reflected" experience requires that we also distinguish between embodying a *sense* of the world habitually and *knowing* its meanings. Schutz's theory of "taken-for-granted," or "typified," knowledge fails to account for the "presence of the past" at the level of sense.

Given the impact that Schutz's theory of taken-for-granted knowledge has had on the definition of phenomenology within sociology, I believe that an alternative approach to habituality suggests a redefinition of phenomenological reflection within the discipline—a redefinition that invites sociology to investigate prereflective experience. It is useful to compare Schutz's and Merleau-Ponty's respective conceptions of the phenomenological reduction to the sphere of "pure subjectivity," since the differences between them relate directly to the contrasting concepts of habit developed by each writer. This chapter compares the philosophies of Schutz and Merleau-Ponty as a basis for further elucidations of the importance of a theory of habitual sense—or what I call *sensitivity*—for phenomenological social theory.

Habit and taken-for-granted knowledge

Edmund Husserl argues for a recovery of the genesis of meaning in human existence. This requires a return to "the things themselves," meaning a return to the pure givenness of phenomena within experience. To reach this level we must suspend from reflection the presuppositions that comprise the common-sense conception of the world, which Husserl refers to as the "natural attitude." Common sense assumes that meaning inheres within ideas, objects, and events as if they lead a "natural existence," independent of experience. I assume, for example, that the black and gold stick in my grasp is in and of itself a "pen." Husserl suggests that in doing so I ignore the constitutive dynamics of my consciousness, without which the stick is at best an unintelligible configuration of molecules. It is important to add that Husserl also wants to set aside the common-sense notion that particular activities of consciousness can exist independent of *intended* objects of consciousness. Consciousness is always, Husserl asserts, *consciousness-of*; that is, it is necessarily an intentional grasp of the world (which could be, Husserl is careful to note, a world given through imagination) (Husserl, 1931).

Husserl argues that Western theorizing has been dominated by the presuppositions of common sense, viewing experience as "merely subjective" and the material, or "objective," world as sensible "in itself" (Husserl, 1970). By contrast, phenomenological philosophy "reduces" itself out of the "common-sense" conception of reality in order to uncover the source of a meaningful world within the intentionality of consciousness, or what Schutz calls the "pure life of consciousness...in and through which the objective world exists for me" (Schutz, 1962b: 123). Husserl contends that phenomenology is the first true transcendental philosophy because it is the one method that uncovers the hitherto unrecognized source of the possibility of philosophy or any form of reflection on the world (Kohák, 1978: 171-172).

Transcendental phenomenology employs a reduction of common sense in order to expose the realm of "pure consciousness." Yet Husserl also discusses another form of phenomenological reflection, which he calls "phenomenological psychology," or the phenomenology of the "mundane" (i.e., ordinary world). Here, instead of ridding reflection of common sense, we focus directly upon it, suspending presuppositions in order to bring them into view. In this way the life-world, which includes anything we take to be "real" by virtue of our presupposing its "objective" sensibility, can be explored. If there were no presuppositions, nothing could exist as "real" as opposed to "imaginary" because nothing could be seen to have meaning "on its own," apart from the necessarily subject-centered act of *constituting* its meaning. Phenomenological psychology explores the constituted reality, the life-world, of experience.

Schutz's applications of phenomenological reflection within sociological theory are an elaboration of phenomenological psychology. He argues that the presuppositions of common sense comprise the background, taken-for-granted knowledge of everyday life. From a transcendental phenomenological viewpoint presuppositions conceal processes of meaning-constitution. Under Schutz's conception of phenomenological psychology they are the taken-for-granted assumptions, or "typifications," that, in his view, provide for an exigent social reality—a familiar world that is, in the language of Sartre, sensible "in-itself." The examination of "ordinary *(mundanen)* social life" must therefore abandon phenomenological philosophy's concern with

> the constituting phenomena as these are studied within the sphere of the...reduction. We are concerned only with the phenomena corresponding to them within the natural attitude. (Schutz, 1967: 43-44)

For Schutz, inhabiting "society" as an insider is contingent upon an "everyday *Epochē*" in the sense that we suspend doubt in the practical, pregiven meanings of the life-world. Furthermore, what is unquestionably self-evident from the actor's standpoint is an accomplishment of his own knowledge: We are "able" as a result of typifications that are virtual "recipes" for achieving typical ends under typical circumstances. The development of these recipes is fundamental to "belonging" to society.

In the essay "The Stranger" (1964a) Schutz posits the ideal type of the immigrant: a cultural newcomer with the objective of "being accepted." By explicating the process through which the newcomer becomes an insider, Schutz means to locate the prerequisites of various traditional sociological notions such as "socialization," "social adjustment," "assimilation," or "enculturation." Schutz suggests that the newcomer lacks the typifications *relevant* to the fulfillment of interests within the new social pattern. The newcomer must acquire knowledge that is immediately and prereflectively operative in the form of "trustworthy recipes for interpreting the social world" (Schutz, 1964a: 95). To be a "member of the in-group" is to be able to look

> in a single glance through the normal social situations occurring to him and...catch immediately the ready-made recipe appropriate to its solution. In those situations his acting shows all the marks of habituality, automatism, and half-consciousness. This is possible because the cultural pattern provides by its recipes typical solutions for typical problems available for typical actors. (Schutz, 1964a: 101-102)

The problem of being an insider is not that of collecting more knowledge *about* the world in order to gain better information about its objective contents. Rather, it is a problem of acquiring typifications that constitute being "at home" in a given cultural pattern, or "scheme," of interpretations. Schutz measures the practical, "schematic" adequacy of sedimented knowledge in terms of decreasing levels of "clarity," "consistency," and "coherence" (Schutz, 1964a: 95, 103). In fact, throughout his writings he conceives of the habitual ground of competent involvement within social reality in terms of an *absence* of the necessity for reflective understanding of the environment and how to act within it.

I contend that conceiving of habituality strictly in terms of the absence of reflection produces, at best, a recognition without explication of the structure of experience. Schutz takes the way that the world exists as "subject matter" for reflection as a model for conceptualizing prereflective sensibility. That is to say, he reveals more about the status of prereflectively familiar phenomena *at the level of reflection* than he does about their immanent character. On the other hand, Merleau-Ponty demonstrates that prereflective experience is of a fundamentally different phenomenological order than reflection. Thus, it is an error to formulate experience according to the logic of reflection. Following Merleau-Ponty, we must begin to explore the prereflective present on its own terms.

Embodied sensitivity

In shifting to the writings of Merleau-Ponty we move to a different understanding of the phenomenological reduction, based upon what he takes to be an increasing belief in Husserl's later writings in the foundational importance of the life-world. The accuracy of Merleau-Ponty's reading of Husserl has been questioned elsewhere and need not be discussed here.[2] Merleau-Ponty himself expresses more of a desire to take his departure from what he sees as the general "movement" of Husserl's thought, admitting that he is "perhaps pushing Husserl further than he wanted to go" (Merleau-Ponty, 1962: 365). In any case, my present concern is with the powerful implications for sociological theory of Merleau-Ponty's reworking of the phenomenological reduction and its aims.

In the *Phenomenology of Perception* Merleau-Ponty suggests that the greatest lesson to be learned from the phenomenological reduction is the impossibility of a "complete reduction" (Merleau-Ponty, 1962: xiv). We can never disengage ourselves from the "hold the world has on us" (Merleau-Ponty, 1962: xx). The reduction brings us to the irreducible interwovenness of person and world in experience. It is this interwovenness, therefore, rather than Husserl's "early" conception of a "pure ego," standing apart from and constituting the world's meanings, that is the locus of transcendental subjectivity.[3] Phenomenology becomes *existential* phenomenology because the foundations of meaning are now discovered within the thickness of present existence, a thickness that antecedes the differentiation between subject and world in reflection.

By adhering to Husserl's theory of a reduced "egological" sphere of meaning-constitution, Schutz eliminates the direct relevance of a phenomenological return to "pure subjectivity" for sociological inquiry. Merleau-Ponty, on the other hand, recovers it by reconceptualizing the subjectivity of the world. He shows that the very differentiation between subject and world is a *posited* distinction—an artifact of reflection—that rests upon their "thorough intertwining" in a situation (Mallin, 1979: 8). In Merleau-Ponty's philosophy the situation thereby "comprises the ontological possibility of every other type of entity" (Mallin, 1979: 8). We no longer view the "reduced sphere" in terms of a meaning-constituting ego, and the life-world—including its social structure—is no longer reduced to being a consequence, albeit one "typified" as "reality," of activity that transcends it.

Mallin notes that Merleau-Ponty does not deny the respective independence of the phenomena of subject and environment to the extent that inherent in each is "the possibility of further situations." Yet we can no longer isolate a "set of pure circumstances" and set them against "subjective activities." Person and world are fundamentally comprehensible within a "situational structure in general" (Mallin, 1979: 15), ruling out the premise of a dualism between "psychic" and "material" orders of existence.

In the context of this "situational structure"—the structure of the life-world experienced prior to reflection—the contact between subject and environment has what Merleau-Ponty calls a *preobjective* status in awareness.[4] For example, I do not typically grasp my pen as an *object* of awareness; rather, it is part of the context of a specific form of awareness: theoretical reflection. Indeed, pressing or waiting to press the pen to the page are, in my case, virtual *preconditions* of theorizing. The pen is rarely a focus of such reflection. My contact with the pen is preobjective in the sense that it is part of the texture of consciousness that posits particular objects of attention.

In his later works Merleau-Ponty refers to the preobjective realm of experience as the "flesh." He emphasizes with renewed force a theme present throughout his writings: the corporeality of the preobjective contact between subject and world.[5] As early as *The Structure of Behavior,*[6] Merleau-Ponty argues that, when stripped of the "common-sense" biases of thought, the description of the world prior to reflection is at once a description of a corporeal complicity between person and environment. It is within this complicity that Merleau-Ponty locates the realm of "pure subjectivity."[7]

> For the player in action the soccer field is not an "object," that is, the ideal term which can give rise to an indefinite multiplicity of perspectival views and remain equivalent under its apparent transformations. It is pervaded with lines of force (the "yard lines"; those which demarcate the "penalty area") and is articulated into sectors (for example, the "openings" between the adversaries) which call for a

certain mode of action and which initiate and guide the action as if the player were unaware of it. The field itself is not given to him, but present as the immanent term of his practical intentions; the player becomes one with it and feels the direction of the "goal," for example, just as immediately as the vertical and the horizontal planes of his own body. It would not be sufficient to say that consciousness inhabits this milieu. At this moment consciousness is nothing other than the dialectic of milieu and action. Each maneuver undertaken by the player modifies the character of the field and establishes new lines of force in which the action in turn unfolds and is accomplished, again altering the phenomenal field. (Merleau-Ponty, 1963: 168-169)

The soccer field is not an object of the player's awareness, and yet awareness and field are inseparable in experience. The playing field is, indeed, operative as a lived context that is "present as the immanent term" of the player's intentional actions. It is, like one's own body, preobjective. Phenomenological reflection brings us to this embeddedness of human awareness within the preobjective texture of the situation.

The return to the preobjective is, consequently, a transcendence of the objectifications of both the human body and the inhabited environment in reflection. On the one hand, we see things in the world around us, but we do not usually perceive the eyes that enable us to see. We do not in the first place "know" our bodies; we have them, are them, and only when we turn to the body in awareness—such as when one's eyes hurt while reading or when referring to it in speech—does it take on the secondary, "presupposed" status of a perceived and known "object." On the other hand, we are necessarily situated in a preobjective world, which is to say, our corporeality extends beyond our own skin. The conception of "myself" as an entity that is detached from the world is a late arrival in experience. I constitute the sense of what I am reading, just as the soccer player constitutes the sense of the movements of others around him, through what Husserl calls an "intentional relation." This relation is itself grounded, however, in an original, preobjective contact with my book. When it is intended as such, reading becomes difficult because the world in which it is possible has receded, or more exactly, the contact between person and environment that sustains that particular intentional action has transformed.

Merleau-Ponty develops a theory of habit in order to explicate the preobjective contact between person and world. Habit is conceived as an essential dynamic of experience, as the latter is grasped through a phenomenological suspension of the natural attitude. Merleau-Ponty's approach thus contrasts sharply with Schutz's effort to conceive a habituality *in terms of* the presuppositions of common sense. For Schutz, presuppositions of experience comprise the taken-for-granted knowledge through which the life-world is sustained as "common" sense, whereas for Merleau-Ponty they are the habitual prejudices of reflective thought.

Schutz fails to see that it is only by virtue of our corporeal inherence within a world *having* sense and significance that its meanings can cohere for knowledge.[8] When Schutz conceives of the habitual foundations of social reality as a "stock of knowledge" (Schutz, 1970; Schutz & Luckmann, 1974), he inverts the phenomenological relationship between having the qualities and intensities of the lived world and knowing its meanings. The meaningfulness of the world is reduced to what we are capable of knowing either explicitly or tacitly. It follows that what Merleau-Ponty calls the "prejudice of determinate being" (Merleau-Ponty, 1962: 51) applies to Schutz's theory of social reality in general and, as I later discuss, to his theory of intersubjectivity in particular: It is interpreted as if it were structured on the basis of habitually sedimented objectifications of consciousness, rather than as a structure of the sensibility and significance "which we carry about inseparably with us before any objectification" (Merleau-Ponty, 1962: 362). Merleau-Ponty wants to escape the theoretical tendency to formulate the intelligibility of the world as if prior to reflection it were ordered by the logic that comprises the formulation. Schutz's theory of habituality exemplifies this tendency by essentially conceiving of the prereflective sensibility of social reality according to the logic of its appearance to reflection.

Merleau-Ponty agrees that involvement in the world is grounded in what Schutz calls habitual "sedimentations" of meaning. In contrast to Schutz, however, Merleau-Ponty seeks to locate habit at the level of our familiarity with the world, prior to its determination into distinct objects of knowledge. Hence, where Schutz equates habit with taken-for-granted knowledge that determines the meanings of situated experience, Merleau-Ponty joins John Dewey in conceiving of habit according to its Latin root *habere*, which means "to have" or "to hold," in order to explicate the embodied, preobjective medium of perceptual awareness (Merleau-Ponty, 1962: 174).

While Merleau-Ponty describes habituality as a nonreflective skill or capacity, he does so only in the context of explicating what he calls, following Husserl, the *operative intentionality* that is "found beneath the intentionality of acts, or thetic intentionality" and is "already at work before any positing or any judgment" (Merleau-Ponty, 1962: 429). Merleau-Ponty describes habituality as intentional, in the nonthetic sense of the term, and in this way remains close to Dewey, who asserts that habit is projective—a predisposition to engage the world. Thus, "even if we think of habits as so many grooves, the power to acquire many and varied grooves denotes high sensitivity, explosiveness" (Dewey, 1929: 281).[9]

The concept of "sensitivity" seems particularly well suited to denoting the operative intentionality of embodied habit. Conceived as sensitivity, habit is the very medium of our involvement in a world that matters prereflectively. Stated differently, through habitual sensitivity a "single tension" (Dewey, 1931; Kestenbaum, 1977) endures between the dispositions of self and qualities of the world.[10] Merleau-Ponty grounds the entanglement of corporeal subject and world in the "high sensitivity" of acquired habit:

> [It] is the body which "understands" in the cultivation of habit. This way of putting it will appear absurd if understanding is subsuming a sense-datum under an idea, and if the body is an object. But the phenomenon of habit is just what prompts us to revise our notion of "understand" and our notion of the body. To understand is to experience the harmony between what we aim at and what is given, between the intention and the performance—and the body is our anchorage in a world....When the typist performs the necessary movements on the typewriter, these movements are governed by an intention, but the intention does not posit the keys as objective locations. It is literally true that the subject who learns to type incorporates the key-bank space into his bodily space...habit has its abode neither in thought nor in the objective body, but in the body as mediator of a world. (Merleau-Ponty, 1962: 144-145)

Habit is therefore a sense-enabling structure of the situation, but is irreducible to determined or determinate behavioral or cognitive schemes. It is properly understood only in terms of the experiential dialectic between lived body and world. "Habit," Merleau-Ponty asserts, "expresses our power of dilating our being in the world" (Merleau-Ponty, 1962: 143). It is our power to have experience as embodied significance, which is the power of our past to unceasingly and preobjectively impregnate and "inform" the present.

Dewey writes: "Through habits formed in intercourse with the world, we also in-habit the world. It becomes a home, and the home is a part of our every experience" (Dewey, 1958: 104). Merleau-Ponty means to center phenomenological attention on what it is to have the world as a "home," or, as Husserl calls it in *Experience and Judgment* (1973), a "field of pregivenness."[11] We are steeped within a familiar world prior to any intentional positing or judgment. The medium of such familiarity is a lived body, which is a "thickness" of sensitivity that not only "orients to" or "intends" the world, but also *has* its qualities and intensities, undergoes and embodies them, each moment thereby "driven into time like a wedge" (Merleau-Ponty, 1962: 393).

Merleau-Ponty hopes to explicate what Husserl calls the "passive synthesis" of time in experience, a formulation "which is clearly not a solution, but merely points to the problem" (Merleau-Ponty, 1962: 419). To form habits is to be an *experienced self*—not in the sense of a static compilation of beliefs, skills, and knowledge, but in the dramatic sense of experience as a dialectic between being and becoming *sensitive* to the qualities and intensities of situations. Hence, the "passive synthesis" of past, present, and future experience is not, Merleau-Ponty asserts,

> the acceptance by us of an alien reality, or a causal action exerted upon us from the outside: It is being encompassed, being in a situation— prior to which we do not exist—which we are perpetually resuming and which is constitutive of us. A spontaneity "acquired" once and for all, and one which "perpetuates itself in being in virtue of its being acquired" [Sartre, *L'Être the le Néant*, 1943: 195] is precisely time and subjectivity. (Merleau-Ponty, 1962: 427)

Merleau-Ponty purposely quotes Sartre out of context in the above passage, noting that for Sartre habitual acquisition is a "monster" that he mentions "only to banish the idea of it." Gila Hayim writes that for Sartre:

> a human being is the sum total of his acts; hence, there is no hidden essence or secret subjectivity. In the context of Sartre's work, existence is defined by and through one's acts. Existence cannot hide behind the pretext of inwardness or *potentia*. One is what one does. (Hayim, 1980: 3)[12]

Merleau-Ponty wants to show that a phenomenological grounding of selfhood in the lived present need not entail a Sartrean commitment to a view of the self as nothingness aside from possible acts. It is precisely the absence of a theory of habit that renders Sartre's position vacuous phenomenologically because there is then no basis within a world continuously opening as *potentia* for feeling and sensing emergent *possibilities* within present experience.

The self is neither naturally predetermined, nor simply a compilation of acts past, present, or future. Rather, it is a transforming (or stagnant)[13] field of embodied sensitivity. Mikel Dufrenne makes this point in different terms when, in explicating the possibility of aesthetic perception, he writes:

> This past which I am gives a density to my being and a penetrating quality to my glance. How would I have any sensation of music if my ear were a mere receptacle for sounds, if it were not informed and, moreover, if it did not allow for the sounds to reverberate and find an echo in this self which I offer them?...I participate in the work [of art] through something in me which is capable of being affected, through the substantial and yet nonmaterial density of a deep and profound self. (Dufrenne, 1973: 404)

Possibilities are not merely "confronted," as Sartre would say; they are "born of habit" (Merleau-Ponty, 1962: 238). They are created within a perpetual dialectic between being "experienced" and presently experiencing the environments that situate us.

Sociality as a foundation of consciousness

Habits are virtual "sedimented situations" (Mallin, 1979: 12), or more specifically, they are the embodied sensitivity that, to use Husserl's term, "protends" situations. We remain perpetually steeped within shifting situations that we simultaneously inhabit and embody the sense of in our habits, thus ensuring that the contact between subject and world is no momentary eruption *in* time, but the very *flesh* of time.[14] It is the embodied interpenetration of past, present, and future circumstances. Dewey's claim that "the things with which a man varies are his natural environment" (Dewey, 1916: 11) applies as much to the tempo of passing moments as passing years. The principle of protentional embodiment remains foundational: The subject's "inherence in a field of time" (Kestenbaum, 1977: 91)[15] is a persistence and transformation of sensitivity to the world.

Our habituality steeps us within and compels us to adjust to perpetually changing conditions of inhabiting the environment. Moments of experience thereby "hang together, are mutually motivating and implicatory" (Merleau-Ponty, 1962: 304). I move my eyes and am not flabbergasted by what, in all objective appearances, is an upheaval in my field of vision (Merleau-Ponty, 1962: 169). The *sense* of the world is not contingent upon positing the meanings of, or "signifying," its features at every turn. That would involve us in an infinite regression of *making* sense, which would rule out any progressive development of ideas in consciousness. We are conscious within situations, our embodied sensitivity providing for our preobjective "cohesion" with the world.

The idea of a "cohesion" of body and world refers to the power of our sensitivity to, so to speak, turn the world in favor of its experientially gripping qualities and to sustain them. The haunting melody of the andante in Brahms' second piano concerto saturates my living room, and my listening body coheres with it as tightly as the soccer player's with his playing field. Yet the andante is not merely a "thing" that I confront from time to time. My sensitivity to flickering and glowing musical themes is an operative form of the cohesion of my body with the world. Hence, the music exists *in habit*; it has manifested itself as an integral aspect of my personal history. The concerto is always an occasion of the moment, but it is also a part of myself that is "played out" as my environment radiates with melody. In fact, Brahms' passages often pulsate at varying levels of intensity within my awareness even when the music isn't "on" (which can either complement or compete with other forms of my attention). My experience of a musical world oscillates between the operative and the active, which is the interchange between the possible and the actual that Dewey calls the drama of habit (Dewey, 1929; Kestenbaum, 1977).

Embodied sensitivity is a precondition of human consciousness in the sense that it establishes the "preliminary presence" (Husserl, 1973: 29) of a field of potential objects of consciousness. This claim establishes a basis for moving from a sociology of knowledge to a phenomenological sociology of sensitivity. Acquired habit can then be conceived purely in terms of the "drama" of the lived present. Explicating the social structure of consciousness is no longer a matter of identifying latent knowledge, because habituality is no longer posited "outside" of or "behind" experience. Habituality is now seen as the lived perpetuation of the contact between self and world.

It is precisely in terms of the acquisition and embodiment of sensitivity that the *sociality* of human existence can be located as a foundational structure of consciousness. When Schutz describes the subject's attachment to a social world in terms of "taken-for-granted knowledge" or "typifications" of everyday life situations, he produces a gloss, as opposed to an elaboration, of the prereflective dynamics of our being immersed within situations that "reverberate" (Husserl, 1973: 110, 122) with the qualities and intensities that simultaneously engage and are engaged by our sensitivity.[16] We must move from the problem of "common-sense knowledge...what people 'know' as 'reality' " (Berger and Luckmann, 1966: 5) to one of embodied sensitivity, thereby explicating social reality at its level of *sense*—the level that is skirted by the reduction of habituality to taken-for-granted knowledge. Schutz brought sociology to the threshold, but the theoretical task remains to push to the interior, of the prereflective sociality of situations. It is with this aim that we now turn to the problem of intersubjectivity.

Chapter Three

The Intersubjective Contact:
The Preobjective Level of Social Life

It is as false to place ourselves in society as an object among other objects, as it is to place society within ourselves as an object of thought, and in both cases the mistake lies in treating the social as an object. We must return to the social with which we are in contact by the mere fact of existing, and which we carry about inseparably with us before any objectification.

Maurice Merleau-Ponty
Phenomenology of Perception

The topic of intersubjectivity is hardly central among the concerns of contemporary social theorists. It can be characterized as one of a group of themes presumed to have little if any relevance to investigations of conditions and processes of social life. A well-known exception is Alfred Schutz's *The Phenomenology of the Social World* (1967), where he observes that the analytical possibility posed by Weber of interpreting social situations at the level of "subjective meaning" for participants turns on the problem of intersubjectivity, or how it is that we orient to and make sense of others as *subjects* of their own experiences. While I reject Schutz's theory of intersubjectivity in favor of one rooted more in the phenomenological philosophy of Merleau-Ponty, I nevertheless follow the intent of Schutz's effort to demonstrate the relevance of the topic of intersubjectivity for sociological theory, by showing that it is presupposed by any conception of the subjective meaning of social life.

Before contrasting Schutz's and Merleau-Ponty's approaches to the problem of intersubjectivity it is important to note Kurt H. Wolff's distinction between the topics of intersubjectivity and intersubjective understanding (Wolff, 1984). The latter refers to the Weberian concern with the adequacy of persons' interpretations of

35

others' experiences, and Schutz's discussion of intersubjectivity is intended primarily as an expansion and refinement of this concern. Husserl is, on the other hand, less concerned with how we can understand one another accurately, in terms of one another's "real" feelings and thoughts, than with establishing the phenomenological grounds for our ability to perceive others as meaning-constituting subjects of their own consciousness, as opposed to mere objects of perception. That is to say, Husserl pays less attention to the problem of intersubjective understanding than to intersubjectivity *as such*— as an essential property of human consciousness.

If we adhere to the analytical distinction between intersubjectivity and intersubjective understanding, then contrasting the philosophies of Schutz and Merleau-Ponty appears problematic at the outset: Merleau-Ponty's focus is aligned more with Husserl's effort to establish that intersubjectivity is grounded in the fundamental structure of experience than with Weber's (and Schutz's) focus on "meaning-adequate interpretation." There are, however, legitimate bases for comparison. It is true that Schutz operates at the level of Weber's concerns in his elaborations of intersubjectivity, but he does so in the context of a *refutation* of Husserl's belief that intersubjectivity is an *essential* structure of consciousness. Schutz accepts Husserl's formulation of the process through which others are perceived as persons, adding that this process is contingent upon "typified" schemes of interpretation. While Merleau-Ponty seeks to deliver on Husserl's promise of defining intersubjectivity as a transcendental phenomenon, he *opposes* Husserl's formulations, and I contend that in doing so he provides grounds for contesting Schutz's claim that typified interpretations are the bases of intersubjective awareness. I particularly want to show how Merleau-Ponty's concept of preobjective habit leads to an identification of embodied, intersubjective sensitivity as an essential experiential feature of human existence.

Intersubjectivity and taken-for-granted knowledge

Husserl claims that if philosophy suspends all presuppositions of the "natural attitude" and returns to the pure "I"—the transcendental ego—of experience, then it discovers our essential human capacity to perceive other bodies as *subjects* in the same sense that we, the perceivers, are subjects. We can do so through the process of "apperceiving" them as "alter egos." Husserl uses the term "apperception" (for which he occasionally substitutes the term "appresentation") in order to distinguish the consciousness of persons from the consciousness of objects. Other persons are *animate* in ways that are, through an apperceptive "pairing" of their bodies with ours, viewed as the experiences of human subjects, rather than the mere motions of objects. Stated differently, the other is perceived as an "alter ego" by virtue of an "apperceptive transfer" of the sense of our own behavior to that perceived in the other (Husserl, 1960).[1]

Schutz argues that Husserl fails to demonstrate a basis for the apperception of others within the phenomenologically reduced sphere of transcendental subjectivity. He contends that Husserl is, in fact, mistaken in believing that the essence of intersubjectivity can be located within this sphere. The concept of "apperception" implies a form of reasoning by analogy. Husserl does not account satisfactorily for how the constituting of meaning in consciousness is projected into a visible body that is, as soon as *perceived*, constituted as such, becoming an observed "exteriority," versus an inner stream of consciousness (Schutz, 1962c; Schutz, 1966b; Carrington, 1979).[2]

In Schutz's view the phenomenological task is not to solve this apparent impasse within the "reduced sphere," but to grasp why no impasse exists within the "natural attitude." Hence, intersubjectivity is properly understood as a problem of "phenomenological psychology," rather than one of transcendental phenomenological philosophy. It is a phenomenon of the world that we take to be "real" by virtue of *presupposing* its meanings (cf. Chapter 2). In everyday experience there is typically no problem in perceiving another person as the subject of a stream of consciousness: The other's body is perceived directly as the medium of the other's feelings and thoughts, and it is usually not necessary to formulate it as such in reflection. Schutz notes that, as a matter of fact, it is only when we do perceive others that it is possible to attend to thoughts and feelings while they occur, since one's own consciousness can only be viewed retrospectively, through reflection. We perceive one another, without conscious predication, as subjects of experience. When we attend to one another simultaneously, we are involved in what Schutz calls the "We-relation" where, through the mutual activities of attending to and being attended to by one another, streams of consciousness are mutually constitutive (Schutz, 1967; Schutz and Luckmann, 1974).[3]

The essay "Making Music Together" is one of Schutz's best elaborations of the We-relation. He argues that in listening to music we actualize the performer's (who himself actualizes the composer's) creation of a particular temporal experience. Two movements of a symphony may last for equal lengths of clock time; yet as *music*, meaning within the context of the listener's or performer's reality, they may differ enormously in their temporal sense, or their "durée," to use Henri Bergson's term. Schutz is claiming that music can be "known" *as music* within immediate experience, but never in reflection, because the latter pulls it out of its unfolding in experiential time. His further point is that it is in the process of having a musical experience that one is "tuned in" to the performer's stream of consciousness. This "tuning in" is, as the central dynamic of the We-relation, "at the foundation of all possible communication" (Schutz, 1964b).[4]

When Schutz discusses intersubjectivity as a prereflective "tuning in" to the consciousness of others, he means to describe social reality from the standpoint of its common-sense acceptance. We believe we "tune in" to another's consciousness because our own interpretations of the other's visible gestures as their consciousness become taken-for-granted and typified. Schutz contends that if we phenomenologically suspend these typifications we confront the fact that a subject's consciousness is *never* available firsthand to outside perception. Only a subject in the world, an "I," can inhabit a stream of consciousness and live its content directly and pre-predicatively, within its original "subjective meaning context." By contrast, a subject's consciousness has meaning for *others* only insofar as they *interpret* the subject's observably discernible acts, placing consciousness within an "objective meaning context" (Schutz, 1967).[5] The analytical problem becomes how, in the face of an acknowledgment of the prereflective level of intersubjective experience, typifications invest social encounters with a kind of practical bypass of the inherently subjective and, thus, potentially private nature of consciousness.

Schutz's analysis centers on our interpretations of what we and others symbolically represent, or "signify," by movements and gestures, but he adds the proposition that these interpretations are based upon underlying, taken-for-granted schemes that obviate the need for reflection. There is at best an "objective probability" that our interpretations of one another's consciousness are accurate. Yet by virtue of acquired schemes of interpretation, this probability becomes, for "all practical purposes," a subjective assurance, or a habitual confidence in our abilities to convey the contents of our consciousness to one another (Schutz, 1967).

The implication of Schutz's argument is that the immediacy of the other's experience to our perceptions, and of ours to his or hers, are illusions, albeit practical ones, supported by habit: What we *really* have before us are not the direct experiences of one another, but mere series of observable "bodily movements" that serve habitually as signs of the "lived experiences lying behind and signified by them" (Schutz, 1967: 100)[6] Hence, we virtually, rather than actually, perceive the other's consciousness. It is virtually the case that we do so because within the "mundane" or "practical" sphere of existence our sedimented "codes of interpretation [direct] us not to the perceived, i.e., the body, but through its medium to the Other's lived experiences themselves" (Schutz, 1932: 101). Yet what we actually communicate with are the other's *representations* of underlying experience. It is only because our interpretations, or what Schutz calls "symbolic-signitive inferences," are sedimented at a level of taken-for-grantedness that we presume direct and unmediated access to the other's subjectivity.

We have seen that Schutz's theory of intersubjectivity takes its departure from Husserl's conception of subjectivity. The lived-through sense and significance of the present is constituted within a subject's unfolding stream of consciousness. Another person's access to that stream is always *mediated* by the symbolism of the subject's object-perceivable body. Actually, the notion of symbolic-signitive inference is simply a refinement of Husserl's idea of the "apperceptive transfer of sense," the central difference being that Schutz locates the possibility of "apperception" outside the reduced sphere of the transcendental ego. Merleau-Ponty contrasts with Schutz by rejecting the idea of apperception altogether, instead conceiving of intersubjectivity as a fundamental dimension of the preobjective corporeality of experience.

Intersubjective sensitivity

In the previous chapter I observed that Merleau-Ponty does not discard the phenomenological notion of transcendental subjectivity, but denies that it is a "pure interiority," or "constituting power," that is "as yet untouched by being and time" (Merleau-Ponty, 1962: v).[7] The notion of a transcendental subject standing apart from and constituting the world is as removed from an accurate location of the foundations of meaning as what Husserl identifies as the error of modern thought ever since Galileo that locates the origins of meaning within the objective environment (Husserl, 1970). The transcendental subject can be no more nor less than a person *situated* within the world. The meanings of the world are, therefore, neither "objectively" self-contained, nor "subjectively" constituted freely, but located within experience—a sustained dialectic between lived body and environment.

With his theory of the lived body Merleau-Ponty rejects the tendency to treat issues of the mind and its "mental processes" independently of those of the body and its "behaviors." The body as lived is the subject incarnate, and only through a contrivance of reflection is consciousness viewed separate from, rather than within, the original, preobjective texture of its body. This emphasis on the preobjective corporeality of inhabiting the world is the point of departure for Merleau-Ponty's theory of intersubjectivity.

It is precisely because of its corporeal texture that consciousness continuously tends to directly and without cognitive mediation reveal itself within a social world. "Subjective meaning" could remain private only on the condition of freezing one's bodily motility in the world. This would, in effect, neutralize any sense an observer might have of a human subject *living* that body. In order to take such an option seriously we would have to conceive of the human subject apart from its possibilities of involvement in the world. For example:

> If I am dealing with a stranger who has as yet not uttered a word, I may well believe that he is an inhabitant of another world in which my own thoughts and actions are unworthy of a place. But let him utter a word, or even make a gesture of impatience, and already he ceases to transcend me: that, then, is his voice, those are his thoughts and that is the realm that I thought inaccessible. Each existence finally transcends the other's only when it remains inactive and rests upon its natural differences....Solipsism would be strictly true only of someone who managed to be tacitly aware of his existence without being or doing anything, which is impossible, since existing is being in and of the world. (Merleau-Ponty, 1962: 361)

Merleau-Ponty means to define intersubjectivity in terms of a theory of experience that pulls "subjectivity" out of the hidden recesses of a constituting mind, placing it, in the "flesh," within the world. Identifying the lived body as an irreducible structure of experience establishes a basis for Merleau-Ponty's opposition to the idea that a person's consciousness is only available to others' perceptions through bodily "representation," as if in the absence of such representation consciousness were the enclosed mental sphere of an individual's private existence. We perceive another's body on the same experiential basis that we have and literally are our own bodies.

When someone looks or sounds "tired," "confused," or "elated," that is, in Dewey's terms, our perceptual *sense*, as opposed to our *signification*, of his or her corporeal situation. To say, as Schutz does, that the other's consciousness is visible to our perceptions only by *interpreting* the other body's symbolic representations of it is as much a distortion as would be the claim that when we think, feel, or perceive we are actually making rapid-fire interpretations of particular movements or sensations of our own bodies. It is clearly absurd to suggest that it is only by quickly interpreting shifts in where my eyes point that I can see. Nevertheless, we are able to *posit* this division between the mind and the body. This freedom of reflection accounts for the modern philosophical error, inspired by the thought of René Descartes, to assume a dissociation of mind and body *prior* to reflection. This assumption guides Schutz's notion of the body signifying an otherwise invisible and "internal" subjective process.

Schutz correctly claims that the accuracy or completeness of our interpretations of what others are aware of is never assured. This lack of assurance can take on significance in our social relationships; we may wonder what is really "on the other's mind." When Merleau-Ponty speaks of the corporeal visibility of consciousness, he refers to an existentially given aspect of the field of consciousness that by no means *exhausts* the field. We are never assured of sharing in the full affective, perceptual, and cognitive thickness of another's awareness and are, consequently, never in the clear of possible wonder, confusion, or doubt about what we see and hear. Likewise, there remains indeterminacy with respect to both the extent and quality of our own visibility to others. We speak of behavior not only conveying but also betraying or distorting our views and feelings. Indeed, as Goffman shows, the visibility of consciousness often escapes intentional control, which is a matter of some concern in circumstances where the nature of a social relationship hinges on the subtlest of impressions.[8]

Yet Schutz takes the problem of interpersonal understanding to be the *basis* for a theory of how we prereflectively experience the other's presence.[9] In this way he circumvents rather than uncovers the structure of intersubjective reality. He misses that the problem of ascertaining exactly what others are aware of is a late arrival in our direct perception of subjects who are conscious, as we are ourselves, through the medium of their lived bodies. Merleau-Ponty writes:

> The other consciousness can be deduced only if the emotional expressions of others are compared and identified with mine, and precise correlations recognized between my physical behavior and my "psychic events." Now the perception of others is anterior to, and the condition of, such observations, the observations do not constitute the perception. A baby of fifteen months opens its mouth if I playfully take one of its fingers between my teeth and pretend to bite it. And yet it has scarcely looked at its face in a glass, and its teeth are not in any case like mine. The fact is that its own mouth and teeth, as it feels them from the inside, are immediately, for it, an apparatus to bite with, and my jaw, as the baby sees it from the outside, is immediately, for it,

capable of the same intentions. "Biting" has immediately, for it, an intersubjective significance. It perceives its intentions in its body, and my body with its own, and thereby my intentions in its own body.... The possibility of another person's being self-evident is owed to the fact that I am not transparent for myself, and that my subjectivity draws its body in its wake. (Merleau-Ponty, 1962: 352)

I am not "transparent for myself" because there is no apodictically self-evident "I" that transcends my existence as an ultimate source of meaning. "Inside and outside are wholly inseparable. The world is wholly inside as I am wholly outside myself" (Merleau-Ponty, 1962: 401).[10] I am from the outset *situated*; I am in an unceasing, preobjective *contact* with the world, which means subjectivity is as much constituted by the world as it is a force of meaning-constitution within it. It is therefore impossible to locate the source of intentions in either an "inner realm" of self or an "outer realm" of world. The source of intentionality is the lived body, which is as "prepersonal" as personal, as "outrun" by the environment inhabited as it is steeped within the inhabitation. That is why, Merleau-Ponty argues, there is room for another's consciousness within my own: The other has no more of a transcendental command and monopoly over the meanings of the world than I do. We can participate in a *shared world* because its possibilities exceed what we as individual forces of intentionality can determine of it.

Locating the experiential "essence" of our perception of another human being is not a matter of how consciousness is conveyed by and identified with observable bodies. The problem is to discern what Merleau-Ponty calls the "intercorporeality" (Merleau-Ponty, 1964b) of social life: the preobjective, situational character of our presence to one another. In the above passage the infant discovers in the adult's body what Merleau-Ponty calls a "miraculous prolongation of its own intentions, a familiar way of dealing with the world" (Merleau-Ponty, 1962: 354). Yet Merleau-Ponty knows it is not enough to say that the infant discovers this as a spectator, witnessing the replication of its own intentions by the other. This would limit the intersubjective significance of the other's body to its observable characteristics, and Merleau-Ponty would be forced into the Husserlian dilemma of accounting for how an analogy is made between one's own lived body and that perceived. Rather, when he says "biting" has an immediate, intersubjective significance, he denotes the inseparability of perceiving another's behavior from undergoing one's own corporeal existence. It is in this preobjective sense of copresence—a "cohesion without concept"—that Merleau-Ponty insists the other person is no "mere bit of behavior in my transcendental field, nor I in his; we are collaborators for each other in consummate reciprocity. Our perspectives merge into each other, and we coexist through a common world" (Merleau-Ponty, 1962: 354).[11]

This idea of a "merging of perspectives" should not be confused with Max Scheler's claim that human beings are born into an undifferentiated "pure psychic givenness"—a "universal stream of consciousness"—that antecedes "self-realization" (Scheler, 1954).[12] It is not that our intersubjectivity "transcends" our subjectivity; rather, Merleau-Ponty conceives of it as a specific and fundamental possibility of a *subject's* experience. When he speaks of the other's body and one's own as "one whole, two sides of one and the same phenomenon" (Merleau-Ponty, 1962: 354), he refers to a particular way for a subject to have contact with a world saturated with the presence of others. This is precisely why Merleau-Ponty's theory of intersubjectivity provides a basis for explicating the foundational *social* dimension of habitual sensitivity. Dewey's assertion that "habits constitute the self" (Dewey, 1922: 25) defines the "self" as a persistence and actualization of possibilities for involvement in the world. Intersubjectivity is an essential context of these possibilities: What Merleau-Ponty shows to be the capacity of consciousness to reveal itself through the body emerges within various situations as a predominant mode of awareness.

Within contexts of social copresence, the corporeal subject lives through an intersubjective sensitivity to the world. Our eyes *gaze* and catch others' gazes; which is to say, *seeing* is intersubjectively sensitive, or structured in ways intrinsic to this sensitivity. Thinking occurs through the modes of speech and gesture; our voices, faces, hands—the various visible aspects of our embodiment—evince our intersubjective habits of awareness. Consciousness, in other words, becomes *expressive*, and this is why Merleau-Ponty asserts that "to express is to become aware of" (Merleau-Ponty, 1964b: 90). Human expression is a specific form, as opposed to a mere representation or signification, of consciousness.[13] The problem is not, then, to discover a relationship *between* expression and consciousness, by which the former apparently "designates" or "clothes" the latter. We must grasp how expression "becomes the presence" of consciousness in a social environment (Merleau-Ponty, 1962: 182), and also how we perceive one another within this medium of sensitivity.[14]

Expression as a medium of consciousness

Expression "premeditates itself" (Merleau-Ponty, 1964b: 18) as an acquired power of the habitual body. Hence, speech or gesture do not exist in a vacuum; they cannot be caught theoretically as experiential phenomena if we restrict our attention to their observable mechanics or content and ignore their situational genesis. To speak or gesture is to engage in "a certain modulation of the body as a being in the world" (Merleau-Ponty, 1962: 403). This is a modulation of sensitivity, or a shift of habit into the key of intercorporeal presence. It is in this way that expression "ends the alternative...between me as subject and the other as object" (Merleau-Ponty, 1973b: 145). Expression is the manner of inhabiting a social world, and the term "intersubjectivity" denotes that self and others are "wholly present in that manner" (Merleau-Ponty, 1964b: 43). We are thus fully absorbed by our sensitivity to our presence for others, and of theirs for us, as Béla Balázs reveals in his discussion of a scene from the D.W. Griffith silent film, "Broken Blossoms":

> The hero of the film is a Chinese merchant. Lillian Gish, playing a beggar-girl who is being pursued by enemies, collapses at his door. The Chinese merchant finds her, carries her into his house and looks after the sick girl. The girl slowly recovers, but her face remains stone-like in its sorrow. "Can't you smile?" the Chinese asks the frightened child who is only just beginning to trust him. "I'll try," says Lillian Gish, picks up a mirror and goes through the motions of a smile, aiding her face muscles with her fingers. The result is a painful, even horrible mask which the girl now turns toward the Chinese merchant. But his kindly friendly eyes bring a real smile to her face. The face itself does not change; but a warm emotion lights it up from inside and an intangible nuance turns the grimace into a real expression. (Balázs, 1979: 295)

I suggest that the face does change, but this change cannot be reduced to either its physical attributes or, therefore, to the "sign-signitive" meanings of these attributes. The change is lived in context; it is an experiential change, discernible by a viewing audience attuned to the intersubjectivity of the situation. The real smile is not a "representation" of an otherwise invisible emotion.[15] It is, rather, the embodiment of an emotion actualized within this particular contact. More precisely, through the smile a certain intensity of a social relationship "presses forth," as Dewey would say, through its "ex-pression" (Dewey, 1958: 64)—through the dynamics of intersubjective sensitivity.

Yet it is difficult to say where social relationships begin and leave off with respect to their sustained impact on our manners, or what Merleau-Ponty sometimes calls "styles," of expression. Our sensitivity to particular forms of intersubjective contact includes, but is not limited to, encounters with or even consciousness of the particular "significant others" in our lives. The expressive body varies with different social relationships in all aspects of linguistic and gestural style, yet these variations intermingle within the "inextricable tangle" that is our involvement with the world and with others (Merleau-Ponty, 1962: 454). It is in this ambiguous sense that social relationships persist as forces of intersubjective sensitivity and, thus, forces of expression. As David Sudnow demonstrates, sensitivity to another's presence may reverberate through the expressive body without any perception of the other as such:

When I play "Moon River," I have before me the presence of Audrey Hepurn in *Breakfast at Tiffany's*.... But Audrey Hepurn does not exist for me as an explicitly visual remembrance.... My remembrance of her is not a separate moment of consciousness. There is no facial image that accompanies my play. It is caressing, and impishness, and huddling under the rain that my hands reach for through the sounds. I am being impish and huddling and caressing in the ways of the body. And the real actress and the real film serve only to instigate the mood which is then sustained by the song itself.... Audrey Hepurn, and that motion picture, and those streets, and that story are built into the sounds of the song that are the ways of my body. (Sudnow, 1979: 52-53)

Virginia Woolf provides another example of the preobjective impact of a social relationship on one's operative sensitivity to the environment. Harvena Richter contends that Woolf's writings "make the act of reading approximate the experience itself" through which the reader is "involved actively in the character's total environment—an *enveloppement* in which all the senses, all central and peripheral feelings are called upon" (Richter, 1970: x). In fiction, meanings are *composed* rather than explicated, so that readers follow the world *becoming meaningful* just as it develops and changes for characters. As composition versus exposition, fiction "tells" us little about experience, which is exactly why Husserl upholds the value of fiction for *phenomenological* exposition:[16] Good fiction can reflect experience in its original form, holding the reader's attention at a level of sense that precedes any conceptual reformulation of "what experience means."

In Woolf's *To the Lighthouse* Mrs. Ramsey puts her daughter Cam to bed, wrapping a shawl around an animal skull that, to Cam's dismay, hangs above her:

> she came back to Cam and laid her head almost flat on the pillow beside Cam's and said how lovely it looked now; how the fairies would love it; it was like a bird's nest; it was a beautiful mountain such as she had seen abroad, with valleys and flowers and bells ringing and birds singing and little goats and antelopes and.... She could see the words echoing as she spoke them rhythmically in Cam's mind, and Cam was repeating after how it was a mountain, a bird's nest, a garden, and there were little antelopes...and Mrs. Ramsey went on speaking still more...rhythmically...raising her head very slowly and speaking more mechanically, until she sat upright and saw that Cam was asleep. (Woolf, 1927: 172)

The mind that is seen to "echo" rhythmically with another's words is not the "psychic" realm that Western philosophy and science traditionally sever from the material world. Rather, it is the "body-mind" (Dewey, 1929: 277) of nontheoretical experience in which "the distinction between subject and world is blurred" (Merleau-Ponty, 1964b: 167). When Merleau-Ponty says that "we who speak do not necessarily know better than those who listen to us what we are expressing" (Merleau-Ponty, 1964b: 91), he refers to the intercorporeality of expression, or the vibrating *style* whereby words, "which considered singly are only inert signs, suddenly swell with a meaning which overflows into the other person when the act of speaking binds them up into a single whole" (Merleau-Ponty, 1964b: 235).

Later in *To the Lighthouse*, many years after her mother's death, Cam is falling asleep while sailing away from their island:

> The island had grown so small that it...looked like the top of a rock which some wave bigger than the rest would cover....But as, just before sleep, things simplify themselves so that only one of all the myriad details has power to assert itself, so she felt, looking drowsily at the island; all those paths and terraces and bedrooms were fading and disappearing, and nothing was left but a pale blue censer swinging rhythmically this way and that across her mind. It was a hanging garden; it was a valley, full of birds, and flowers, and antelopes.... She was falling asleep. (Woolf, 1927: 303)

What the reader of Woolf's text can "keep in mind" over the span of 130 pages provides knowledge of what, for the characters themselves, is *had* without being *known*. The text is a window onto the impact of one person's expressive style within another's experience. Without recalling her mother as an object of awareness Cam's perception embodies her operative sensitivity to an environment that is saturated with her mother's presence. This is possible because even in life Mrs. Ramsey was always more than an object of Cam's consciousness. It is not, strictly speaking, other persons, but rather their and our *copresence*—the intercorporeality of our shared environment—that matters to us and "impresses" us habitually. In the final analysis, the live, physical presence of others renders their influence no less ambiguous than it is in their temporary or even permanent absence. We inhabit an intersubjective "swell of meaning" in either case and embody the sensitivity that "presses forth" through our styles of perception and expression.

Our transcendental subjectivity is, at once, intersubjective, at least in part because we cannot freeze in space and time, walled up within our bodies as if the latter were not in the world. We are creatures of habit and are therein doomed by "force of habit" to a saturation with and adjustments to the incessantly transforming situations of the inhabited world. Our lives are interwoven with others who are not mere objects of consciousness, but fields of sensitivity that respond as spontaneously to their visibility as we do. Together we are situated and situational, or in Merleau-Ponty's terms we are "instituted" by and also "institute" (Merleau-Ponty, 1970) the styles that steep us within the world, but elude our awareness, precisely because they *are* our awareness—the "media" of awareness (Dewey, 1958: 63)—in a social world.[17]

If the other is in the first instance no object, but, as we sometimes say, a "force of presence," then what of the "self?" Sociological theory has been dominated by the idea that in order to be a self "for myself," in order to have an "identity," I must realize that I am an object of others' awareness. This idea presupposes that the other person is fundamentally an object (albeit a "subject") of my thetic consciousness—an *interpretandum*—for whom I can only be the same. We are now poised to challenge such a presupposition—and with it the reliance on the concept of "self-objectification" for a sociological account of the structure of what it is "to be luminous for oneself" (Sartre, 1967: 123).

Chapter Four

The Experience of Self:
Sensitivity and Reflexive Awareness

There seems to be no agent more effective than another person in
bringing a world for oneself alive or, by a glance, a gesture, or a
remark, shriveling up the reality in which one is lodged.

Erving Goffman
Encounters

It is not at all true that we are more personal as we are more
individualized...the essential element of the personality is the
social part of us.

Emile Durkheim
The Elementary Forms of Religious Life

When Emile Durkheim insisted on the social essence of what it
means to have a "personality" (Durkheim, 1947), he helped set off a
tradition of claiming the social specificity of what might otherwise
be seen as the most nonsocial of phenomena: the "self." Owing
largely to the writings of Charles H. Cooley and George H. Mead,
Durkheim's maxim has developed into the view, held generally
within sociology, that one's "self" is actually a range of possibilities
of manner and appearance that are contingent upon changes in
social circumstances. The ways that we behave and express
ourselves—from the language we use in our speech to the subtlest
aspects of gesture, intonation, and bodily posture—are social
phenomena that vary with social settings and social relationships.
Cooley and Mead both argue that the variable nature of the self
is comprehensible in terms of the social structure of *reflexive*

51

awareness.[1] In *Human Nature and the Social Order* (1922) Cooley argues that the self emerges within our consciousness through a process of interpretation in which others' perceptions of us serve as a "looking glass" for judging ourselves. This process is observable insofar as it is presupposed in the use of first-person singular pronouns, rendering the self as tangible and, hence, available for sociological investigation as any other identifiable belief or idea.[2] Mead adds what is already presupposed by Cooley: It is through self-objectification—taking ourselves as objects of others' perceptions and attitudes—that we "appear as selves in our conduct" (Mead, 1932: 185). He and the "symbolic interactionists" that followed him argue essentially that this process of self-awareness becomes "embedded" in the form of *roles* through which we meet the expectations of others within particular social settings and relationships.[3] We must virtually "be others," Mead asserts, "if we are to be ourselves" (Mead, 1932: 194).

This chapter elaborates upon Cooley's and Mead's contention that a sociological theory of self is essentially an explication of the dynamics of reflexive awareness. However, I reject the reduction of such awareness to the phenomenon of *self-objectification.* This reduction rests, once again, upon the fundamental presupposition in Western philosophy and science of an a priori separation between subject and world. When we break free of this presupposition, we discover a dimension of reflexivity that is experientially foundational to positing oneself as an object of awareness. In prereflective experience the self figures into awareness, but not primarily, much less necessarily, as an entity that is disengaged from the inhabited world.

It is worth noting that Cooley was more aware than Mead of the need to ground a theory of self-awareness in nonreflective experience. Cooley approached this problem by claiming the existence of a realm of instincts and impulses, which he termed "self-feelings," that "drive" the self to reflexive awareness and assertions of its own interests within social settings. For Cooley, "primitive" self-feelings are preconditions of self-awareness, and he argues this point on both developmental and motivational grounds.

Cooley argues that self-feelings are developmental prerequisites for a child's acquisition of the capacity for self-awareness, as the latter is embodied in the use of first-person singular pronouns. These feelings have their "instinctive" forms of expression; for example, the infant cries for the satisfaction of its hunger. The infant also develops a feel for itself as an influence on others, discovering possibilities of manipulating its own emotional expressions, as in the case of "pouting." The child comes to see others engaged in forms of expression that are already familiar to him as his own. Since these exhibitions are commonly accompanied and refined by the terms "I," "me," or "mine," it is "natural that she [Cooley's daughter] should adopt these words as names for a frequent and vivid experience with which she was already familiar in her own case and had learned to attribute to others" (Cooley, 1922: 191).[4]

Cooley further suggests that self-awareness is itself a primarily affective experience in which specific sentiments emerge out of the more "primitive" realm of self-feeling. It is in this sense that self-feeling persists as the motivating force behind the reflexivity that is exhibited in the use of first-person pronouns within present experience. Cooley writes:

> Concrete self-feeling, as it exists in mature persons, is a whole made up of...various sentiments, along with a good deal of primitive emotion not thus broken up. It partakes fully of the general development of the mind, but never loses that peculiar gusto of appropriation that causes us to name a thought with a first-personal pronoun. (Cooley, 1922: 171)

Mead rejects Cooley's notion of "self-feeling," suggesting that Cooley buys into a solipsistic view of human reality, or the "traditional assumption of psychology [that] the content of experience is entirely individual and not in any measure to be primarily accounted for in social terms..." (Mead, 1934: 224). By locating the self in an instinctive and individual realm of feelings, Cooley has, in Mead's view, contradicted his own insight into the *social* conditions of self-awareness. Mead argues that feelings existing prior to consciousness of one's existence for others are not experiences of a self, but of a human organism that has developed no self. While one may "adjust himself unconsciously to those about him," this occurs at the level of a "bare organic response" (Mead, 1934: 175). For Mead, the self is cognitive: There can be no sense of self without recognizing one's manner and appearance as objects of others' interpretations. What these interpretations are is discernible only by knowing others' linguistic and bodily gestures as signs of interpretations.

Mead is clearly justified to contend that Cooley's theory of instinctive self-feeling represents a retreat into the realm of speculative psychology. Nevertheless, Cooley comes closer than Mead to seeing that any notion of the awareness of self requires explication of its prereflective context.[5] What Cooley fails to see is that the prereflective foundation of self-awareness is not some set of natural, inborn drives; it is *social*. We are sensitive to our own presence in the world prior to being "objects to ourselves" in awareness, and this sensitivity is an intersubjective phenomenon; it is a habitual aspect of our corporeal contact with one another. Reflexivity is, more specifically, an inherently *expressive* habit. Through gesture and speech we not only inhabit contexts of social copresence, but also undergo the force of our own corporeality within them. This chapter explores the reflexive sensitivity of expression in order to locate the awareness of "self" within the "immediate and immanent meaning" of social situations.

I develop my argument initially with a discussion of Erving Goffman's theory of "impression management." This theory enabled Goffman to provide what are perhaps the most comprehensive applications of Cooley's and Mead's theme of the social structure of self-awareness to studies of social events. I am particularly interested in the suggestion scattered throughout Goffman's writings that impression management is not necessarily, or even typically, a *reflective* activity, but one that often occurs "spontaneously" with "unthinking ease" (Goffman, 1959: 75). Goffman does not see that the notion of nonreflective impression management poses a challenge to the reliance on the principle of objectification for understanding the experience of self. His failure to recognize this bears directly upon what might be termed the experiential adequacy of how he interprets his own examples of reflexive conduct. I shall use my criticism of Goffman as a point of departure for delineating the embodiment of reflexive sensitivity in expression.

Self-awareness and spontaneous involvement

How we "define" (Thomas, 1923), or "frame" (Goffman, 1961a: 20; Goffman, 1974: 10-11) social situations is, for Goffman, largely a consequence of our alertness to emergent possibilities of positive or negative impressions of ourselves as reflected by the actual or imagined responses of others. Goffman is famous for providing examples of how we communicate what sorts of individuals we "really" are or are not. The ironic tone of his writings originates with his contention that it is precisely in the context of "impression management" that we "appear as 'selves' in our conduct" (Mead, 1932: 185). Hence, Goffman's work serves to expand Mead's notion of "self-objectification" by locating it as a central ingredient of involvement within social environments.

In order to exhibit good intentions and character we struggle to demonstrate that we share the same values and interactional expectations as others within particular settings. This is essential to what Goffman takes to be the situational character of the phenomenon of "self." It follows that when one's adherence to a common "definition of the situation" is rendered observably questionable by some transgression, the transgressor will be compelled to take measures to demonstrate good will in order to "save face," thereby presenting who he "really is." For example, in *Relations in Public* Goffman notes that an

> individual entering a wrong room where a meeting is in progress may screw up his face and upper body into a comment on his act and ever so quickly withdraw and close the door after him, managing to tiptoe with his face and upper trunk. (Goffman, 1971: 133)[6]

This is one of the many examples Goffman uses to support his contention in *The Presentation of Self in Everyday Life* that impression management is essentially a process of controlling one's "expressions given-off." Expressions given-off consist of the behavior that others take to be noncommunicative on the part of the actor and, for this very reason, revealing of the actor's "true"—

meaning nonself-conscious and, thus, inadvertently "exposed"—character and disposition (Goffman, 1959).[7] The intruder "screws up his face and upper body" without displaying an awareness of doing so. In this way he uses expressions given-off as a medium to communicate his character and does so seemingly without intention in order to avoid being judged as "phony" or "insincere."

The intruder nonverbally "comments on his act," meaning that he virtually "splits himself in two" (Goffman, 1971: 113). He thereby dissociates himself from the discreditable features of previous behavior and, thus, from the self he does not want to be seen as—perhaps rude, or worse, psychologically disturbed. Goffman calls this prevention of negative impressions "remedial work": The intruder subtly admonishes himself, letting his chagrin speak for itself, "enabling him thus to clarify the character and legitimacy of what it is he is about" (Goffman, 1971: 125).

With his notion of our concealed manipulation of others' impressions, Goffman can be viewed to be building upon Simmel's idea that we "play at" society through the interactional art of "sociability." Certainly, Goffman's notion of managed expressions given-off recalls Simmel's contention that sociability is essentially a "doing as if." Yet whereas Goffman finds such maneuvering to represent the individual's concern for and orientation to self, for Simmel sociability is the means by which we reduce the impact of "personal traits" on the course of social interaction. Simmel writes:

> the purely and deeply personal traits of one's life, character, mood, and fate must...be eliminated as factors in sociability. It is tactless, because it militates against interaction which monopolizes sociability, to display merely personal moods of depression, excitement, despondency—in brief, the light and darkness of one's most intimate life. (Simmel, 1950: 46)

Goffman would not disagree, but he adds that it is precisely through expressions produced *as if* they are non-intentional and, thus, nonself-conscious, that the individual works to control how others view him *personally*, in terms of his "real self."[8]

The assumption of our ongoing orientation to what we are or might be from any witnesses' points of view permeates all of Goffman's examples of the tacit expression of self. This is not to suggest that Goffman reduces the individual to a "contemplating head"—one who is perpetually reflective and making sense of his conditions only through reflection (Kosík, 1976: 1). Actually, Goffman never explicitly addresses the status of self-reflexive conduct in awareness, preferring simply to warn the reader that his accounts of human experience are often more metaphorical than literal.[9] In *The Presentation of Self in Everyday Life* he asserts that the tendency of members of Anglo-American culture to see "real performances" as unintentional and lacking in self-consciousness is what has to be exposed as a myth by sociological analysis (Goffman, 1959: 70). Yet just five pages later, Goffman refers to the "unthinking ease" with which presentations of self appropriate to particular social situations are sustained. In fact, at various points in his writings Goffman appears to distinguish between the self-protective functions of gestures and the *self-consciousness* required for their use.

In *Encounters* Goffman discusses at length the importance of "spontaneous involvement" in social interaction. Spontaneous involvement is the engrossment through which individuals are "infused" within social encounters "in a manner quite different from the way an ideally rational player commits his side to a position in an ideally abstract game" (Goffman, 1961a: 38). It is only by maintaining spontaneous involvement within the central focus of attention in an encounter that others can perceive what a person "is and what his intentions are" (Goffman, 1961a: 40). In the following passage Goffman asserts that spontaneous involvement in the social encounter is the basis for a sense of "reality":

> [It] confirms the reality of the world...and the unreality of other potential worlds—and it is upon these confirmations that the stability of immediate definitions of the situation depends (Goffman, 1961a: 40)

It is important to note that although Goffman sees spontaneity as a *performance*—essential to fostering favorable impressions of oneself—he denies that this means it is merely an appearance in the sense of a self-conscious "show":

> spontaneous involvement seems to be least subject to conscious control—for to be concerned about being spontaneously involved in

some activity is necessarily to be spontaneously involved in the concern, not the activity. (Goffman, 1961a: 44)

I have already noted Goffman's central proposition that successful impression management requires an *appearance* of spontaneity. In order for the intruder in the earlier example to display an absence of negative characterological traits, his "expressions given-off" must appear to occur without concern for the possibility of being ascribed these traits. After *Encounters* it seems we must add that the *appearance* of spontaneous gesturing and the *actuality* of spontaneity are one and the same, lest the intruder be "spontaneously involved in the concern, not the activity." In this sense Goffman does not intend to make anything more than *functional* claims about impression management. We must *appear* spontaneous in managing the impressions of others, and we do so by in fact *being* spontaneous. The theory of impression management is therefore more about what is achieved through the dynamics of interaction than what we are actually aware of doing while we interact.

My interpretation of Goffman's analytical intentions is confirmed by his discussion of "ritualization" in *Forms of Talk*, his last published book. Goffman observes, as he does throughout his writings, that various apparently noncommunicative, "physical" gestures—such as throat-clearing, blinking, coughing, or pausing to think—serve important communicative functions within interaction. Goffman then takes up the theme of spontaneity, arguing that after we grow competent in the interactional use of these various gestures they become "ritualized...with no felt contrivance" (Goffman, 1981a: 3). Hence.

> The purpose and function of these displays cannot...be caught by the term "expression," but only by closely examining the consequence each...gesture commonly has in samples of actual occurrences—with due consideration to the sorts of things that might be conveyed in the context had no such gestures been offered. (Goffman, 1981a: 3)

The "displays that cannot be caught by the term 'expression' " are precisely what Goffman referred to twenty-two years earlier as the covertly displayed "expressions given-off" that lie at the heart of impression management. This does not mean that Goffman has retreated from his theory of impression management; he simply wants to make the following methodological point: Since the behaviors to which he wants to attribute dramaturgical meaning are often spontaneous and nonreflective, he withdraws any claim to catching their experiential immediacy. Rather than trying to grasp the sense of gesturing in the context of socially situated experience, Goffman posits its "consequences" within models designed to conform to the logic of self-objectification. That is to say, Goffman, in effect, characterizes gestures *as if* they were motivated and guided by a consciousness of self.[10] He thereby leaves himself open to Merleau-Ponty's charge of "intellectualizing" human experience (Merleau-Ponty, 1962). In Pierre Bourdieu's terms Goffman "slips from a model of reality to the reality of the model" (Bourdieu, 1977: 29).

Reflexive sensitivity

The idea of ritualization represents Goffman's reassessment of the relationship between his analytical ascriptions of significance to the events that he describes and the lived significance of these events for participants. Indeed, his failure to reconcile self-conscious conduct and spontaneity amounts to a failure to do theoretical justice to his own descriptions of social life. Goffman's descriptions are famous within sociology for their special capacity to provide the reader with the feeling that his own conduct is being illuminated (Giddens, 1981: 163-164).[11] I suggest that the evocative power of these descriptions lies largely in their exposure of the lived intensity of immediate experience within social situations. Yet this intensity is skirted, not penetrated, by the theoretical premise of self-objectification. Hence, despite Goffman's adherence to this premise, his descriptions give credence to a theory of the preobjective dimension of reflexivity within social situations. His analytical access to this dimension is blocked, however, by his misunderstanding of the phenomenon of *expression*.

In the previous example of an unintended intrusion on a meeting in progress Goffman describes the intruder's facial contortions and quick exit, "managing to tiptoe with his face and upper trunk" (Goffman, 1971: 133). Goffman means to acknowledge the absence of self-conscious mediation in such behavior when he suggests that it "cannot be caught by the term 'expression.' " What Goffman presupposes is that expression is an execution of otherwise unexpressed intentions. In other words, expression is taken as a *representation* of an underlying consciousness.

Earlier I argued that such a notion of expression derives from the deeper presupposition that separates mind from body. By rejecting this presupposition, we can recover the intrinsic corporeality of consciousness, which is the lived body as the preobjective medium of our inherence in the world. Yet this body is also our *visibility*, a fact that we cannot help but grow sensitive to in our repeated contacts with one another. Merleau-Ponty asserts that the "body proper is a premonition of the other person" (Merleau-Ponty, 1964b: 175). We are sensitive to the intersubjectivity of our existence, and this sensitivity is actualized in gesture and speech. Expressions are not, therefore, mere "representations" of our consciousness; they are the acquired *media* of consciousness in a pervasively social world.

The concept of expression as a preobjective medium of consciousness allows us to view the intruder's "spontaneous involvement" as more than a physiological response to environmental stimuli, while also avoiding the trappings of intellectualism, where interpretations are constructed that are more appropriate to understanding the logic of reflection upon experience than experience itself.[12] The intruder's conduct is *expressive*, not merely as body movements that are "given-off" for others to view, but as the corporeal sense of inhabiting this situation. When he "screws up" and "tiptoes with" his face and upper body, he simultaneously escapes from a place where he does not belong and withdraws from the visibility of his own existence. He thereby at once embodies and reveals to others a sensitivity to the environment's *resistance* to any interpenetration of his own presence with that of others. The preobjective cohesion between those who belong in the meeting is thus exposed as something of a situational repellent to others who might intrude.[13]

Yet only an intersubjectively *experienced* self, only a corporeal subject who is sensitive to the pathways and barriers to contact with others, can embody and, thus, reveal bodily—that is, *express*—a sense of being unwelcome. The intruder's movements are responses to his own presence within a social situation, but at a level prior to self-objectification. Hence, the "self" that "appears" within the intruder's conduct is no object; it is the lived force of his own presence within an intercorporeal situation.

Thus, even in the case of inadvertent and discordant interactional contact, it is to the preobjective texture of this contact that we must turn in order to locate its fundamentally social structure. The very notions of an interactional "violation," its "remedy" or "repair," and the self that is "on the line" during the entire process are conceptual constructions—through either personal consideration or analytical formulation—of a situation the sense of which is not originally one of *concept*, but of the *body*, or more precisely the intersubjectively habitual body.[14]

The preobjective experience of self

The reduction of the phenomenon of self to an object of knowledge is central to Cooley's and Mead's theories of self-awareness, as well as to their elaboration within sociology, most explicitly by symbolic interactionists. This reduction has provided the lasting value of Cooley's and Mead's theories because it manifests the fundamental, Western analytical presupposition of a world of determinate objects. The self is presumed to be originally what reflection has made of it: An observable datum, resting within a world of objects; it is now a thing the existence of which can continue to be identified empirically.

When we break free of this presupposition, we are forced to recognize the intersubjective depth of social interaction; it is a preobjectively felt presence of person-with-others and not merely an exchange between producers and recipients of verbal utterances and nonverbal cues. Just as the orchestra is guided by the conductor's inhabitation of, and not mere "response to," their playing, so is our contact with others also expression *conducted* by the perceived force of our presence echoing through their expressive bodies. The environments we inhabit are pregnant with our speaking and gesturing. This is why we can never be simply "objects to ourselves": Even in our most reflective moments of self-consciousness—such as when remembering how we "must have looked" to others—we live through (if only vicariously through recollection) the preobjective power of our presence within a social world.

Self-awareness is, in short, a particular way of taking thought of a situation. The "self" becomes objectified only through a reflective disengagement from the social situation, as when we speak *about* ourselves, positing our own "behaviors," "psychic states," or "traits" as topics of conversation. It is only apart from a person's prereflective standpoint that the focus of self-awareness can be claimed to be a "subject" separate from a "world" and thereby crammed conceptually within the borders of a human being's skin. If we place the person back at the perspectival locus of the process, then the "self" of self-awareness is no more contained by the walls of the physical body than is experience itself.

The "self" is not an object for the same reason that the "other" cannot be analytically reduced to being an object of interpretation: Both self and other originate and endure within a nonreflective cohesion between body and world. We can, therefore, remain convinced of the fundamentally social character of self-awareness without following the symbolic interactionists in reducing the latter to a process of symbolic representation and interpretation. I see myself reflected in others only insofar as my impact on their situation qualifies *my* present and situates who I am in the process.[15]

James Agee provides a dramatic illustration of the experiential texture of self-awareness when he describes an encounter with a black couple in the deep South during the Depression. Agee's example leads us into the concerns of the next chapter by forcing us to recognize that the inhabitation of social settings is as much a matter of the "macro" histories of those settings as it is of the individual's embodiment of sensitivity. The problem is to establish the relationship between these two levels of history and to see that, phenomenologically, neither can be adequately understood apart from the other. We begin with Agee jogging after the couple to ask them a question, never suspecting the fear that the approach of a white man on an isolated road could evoke:

> At the sound of the twist of my shoe in the gravel, the young woman's whole body was jerked down tight as a fist into a crouch from which immediately, the rear foot skidding in the loose stone so that she nearly

fell, like a kicked cow scrambling out of a creek, eyes crazy, chin stretched tight, she sprang forward into the first motions of a running not human but that of a suddenly terrified wild animal. In this same instant the young man froze, the emblems of sense in his wild face wide open toward me, his right hand stiff toward the girl who, after a few strides, her consciousness overtaking her reflex, shambled to a stop and stood, not straight but sick, as if hung from a hook in the spine of the will not to fall for weakness, while he hurried to her and put his hand on her flowered shoulder and, inclining his head forward and sidewise as if listening, spoke with her, and they lifted, and watched me while, shaking my head, and raising my hand palm outward, I came up to them (not trotting) and stopped a yard short of where they, closely, not touching now, stood, and said, still shaking my head *(No; no; oh, Jesus, no, no, no!)* and looking into their eyes; at the man, who was not knowing what to do, and at the girl, whose eyes were lined with tears, and who was trying so hard to subdue the shaking in her breath, and whose heart I could feel, though not hear, blasting as if it were my whole body, and I trying in some fool way to keep it somehow relatively light, because I could not bear that they should receive from me any added reflection of the shattering of their grace and dignity, and of the nakedness and depth and meaning of their fear, and of my horror and pity and self-hatred; and so, smiling, and so distressed that I wanted only that they should be restored, and should know I was their friend, and that I might melt from existence: "I'm *very sorry!* I'm *very* sorry if I scared you! I didn't mean to scare you at all. I wouldn't have done any such thing for anything."

They just kept looking at me. There was no more for them to say than for me. The least I could have done was to throw myself flat on my face and embrace and kiss their feet. That impulse took hold of me so powerfully, from my whole body, not by thought, that I caught myself from doing it exactly and as scarcely as you snatch yourself from jumping from a sheer height: here, with the realization that it would have frightened them still worse (to say nothing of me) and would have been still less explicable; so that I stood and looked into their eyes and loved them, and wished to God I was dead. After a little the man got back his voice, his eyes grew a little easier, and he said without conviction that that was all right and that I hadn't scared her. She shook her head slowly, her eyes on me; she did not yet trust her voice. Their faces were secret, soft, utterly without trust of me, and utterly without understanding; and they had to stand here now and hear what

I was saying, because in that country no negro safely walks away from a white man, or even appears not to listen while he is talking, and because I could not walk away abruptly, and relieve them of me, without still worse a crime against nature than the one I had committed, and the second I was committing by staying, and holding them. And so, and in this horrid grinning of faked casualness, I gave them a better reason why I had followed them than to frighten them, asked what I had followed them to ask; they said the thing it is usually safest for negroes to say, that they did not know; I thanked them very much, and was seized once more and beyond resistance with the wish to clarify and set right, so that again, with my eyes and smile wretched and out of key with all I was able to say, I said I was awfully sorry if I had bothered them; but they only retreated still more profoundly behind their faces, their eyes watching mine as if awaiting any sudden move they must ward, and the young man said again that that was all right, and I nodded, and turned away from them, and walked down the road without looking back. (Agee, 1960: 39-41)

Merleau-Ponty writes that "as the parts of my body together comprise a system, so my body and the other person's are one whole, two sides of one and the same phenomenon" (Merleau-Ponty, 1962: 354). Agee's approach envelops this couple's experience; their bodies vibrate with it visibly. He feels the woman's heart blasting through himself because no less an apparently "inner sanctum" than the beating heart is saturated by and saturating of the world that is lived by more than one habitual body. The couple's fear is not some internal, psychic event that can only be "symbolized" and then "read" by the other. Their fear is what their situation is at this instant, but this is a situation that is created by, and only in the context of, an intercorporeal present. An atmosphere of terror is "constituted" by neither them nor Agee because it is no mere object of consciousness; it is a lived foundation of consciousness, instituted by this intersubjective contact and thereby instituting what Agee and this couple are as intersubjectively sensitive beings in this world.

Agee's presence terrifies the couple, and that is precisely why he too can be steeped within their terror. It is through *inhabiting* his impact on the couple's world, therefore, and not simply by "judging" himself as an interpreted "personality" or "character," that Agee becomes self-conscious. Interestingly enough, he first "speaks" to the couple without any reference to "himself": "shaking my head *(No; no; Oh, Jesus, no, no, no!)."* After this his communication becomes explicitly self-referenced: " 'I'm *very sorry!*...I didn't mean to scare you at all. I wouldn't have done any such thing for anything.' " Yet the preobjective intensity of the situation does not "give way" to self-consciousness as if thought could separate from its body; rather, this intensity endures as the corporeality of self-consciousness. Agee *perceives* the couple's "view of him" *in the context* of his sensitivity to the pervasiveness of his presence within this social environment. That sensitivity is the precondition for his reflections on what he "means to them," and it provides the experiential ground for knowing himself, for his "self-concept" in the Southern world.

Nevertheless, there is clearly a profound discrepancy between who Agee is within his own awareness and how the couple views him. Indeed, it appears that Agee's impact on the couple's experience violates more than flows from his initial sense of their world and his place within it. The couple's experience of Agee's presence is not simply a matter of their interactional exchange with him, however, and so interaction analysis alone could not account for the social structure of the encounter. It would not be enough to say, as Goffman might for instance, that the couple "misreads" the meanings of Agee's conduct, thereby "misframing" his character. When Agee's shoe "twists" in the gravel, the woman instantly breaks into the first motions of running. It is the thrust of his approach within a world that is at once structured *for* her, as her *culture*, and embodied *by* her, as her *sensitivity*, that institutes a situation that in large part occasions, rather than being occasioned by, the interactional methods or strategies of the moment.

Agee cannot compel the couple to see him for what he "really" is because he cannot break the dialectic between "objective" and "personal" history that conditions what he is for them even before they meet. The couple is "at home" within this sociohistorically conditioned environment, and they can no more escape the terrifying impact of this white man's presence than they can leave behind their own bodies. By contrast, the possibility and actuality of a white man's presence in the deep South have cultural meanings that exceed what Agee is historically sensitive to being for others. He lacks familiarity with his own intersubjective power in this culture. He is not at home in the couple's world—the very world that now saturates his experience and institutes his social impact—and is confronted with the self-conscious absurdity of trying to demonstrate that fact, attempting to exhibit his nonallegiance to the very world that situates his and the couple's habitual beings.

Agee's example teaches us that experience is a dialectic between two histories, the individual's and the setting's; yet an individual's history is necessarily a history of inhabited social settings, and a social setting's is the history of the individuals who inhabit it. The single historicity of experience is one of sensitivity that is as "objective" as it is "subjective" and thereby manifests the forces of two pasts. We must conceive of the self as a "meeting of two pasts" (Bourdieu, 1981: 315) in order to reach a fuller understanding of the sensitivity that immerses us within the sociality of our world.

Chapter Five

The Disposition of Social Position:
Habitus and Sensitivity

> When the same history inhabits both habitus and habitat, both
> dispositions and position, the king and his court, the employer
> and his firm, the bishop and his see, history in a sense com-
> municates with itself, is reflected in its own image.
>
> Pierre Bourdieu
"Men and Machines"

Within sociology the division between "micro" and "macro"
theoretical concerns is predicated on the apparently obvious
distinction between sociohistorically structured settings and the
dynamics of individuals' activities within them.[1] The obviousness of
this distinction rests upon the presumption in Western philosophy
and science of a dualism between subject and world. The previous
chapters have set aside this presumption in order to conceptualize
the social character of prereflective experience. At this level of
conceptualization the segregation of "micro" and "macro" concerns
collapses: We can no longer take as an unquestioned point of
departure the theoretical split between social environments and
what persons do, think, and feel within them.

It cannot be denied that possibilities of involvement within any
social setting are shaped by forces that both antecede and persist
long after any one person's existence. Yet this does not mean that
these forces are not *personal*—that they are not matters of the
qualitative immediacy of the world in experience. Grounding the
sociality of human existence within the structure of experience does
not ipso facto reduce social meaning to a matter of intentional
constitution. Consciousness exists only within a world that is
already *instituted* preobjectively by embodied sensitivity. Sensi-

67

tivity is personal, but it is not private: Through sensitivity we are immersed within and habitually oriented to the presence of others. This chapter argues that the *genesis* of sensitivity is also not private, but rather is conditioned by forces within the social environment that are themselves operative only through such conditioning.

A precedent for locating the sociohistorical conditions of human existence within the structure of habit is established in the work of Pierre Bourdieu. Bourdieu develops a theory of *habitus* in order to conceive of the social structure of the subject-environment relationship as an "intentionless," historically emergent phenomenon, but one that is comprehended adequately only in terms of the embodied "dispositions" of individuals. Bourdieu defines habitus as a "system of durable, transposable dispositions" (Bourdieu, 1977: 72). Habitus renders the environment familiar, furnishing its "practical sense"[2] from the standpoint of a social position (as social position is structured by such "objective factors" as race, age, class, and gender). I will use Bourdieu's concept of habitus to develop a theoretical perspective that attends simultaneously to the qualitative immediacy of experience and the rootedness of experience within historically conditioned environments.

Bourdieu is himself not concerned with the dynamics of immediate experience; in fact, he more or less views such a concern as a retreat into a form of "subjectivism" that fails to account for the sociohistorical determinates of human existence. In *Outline of a Theory of Practice* Bourdieu writes:

> What is radically excluded from phenomenological analysis of the "general thesis of the natural standpoint" which is constitutive of "primary experience" of the social world is the question of the economic and social conditions of the *belief* which consists in "taking the factworld *(Wirklichkeit)* just as it gives itself." (Bourdieu, 1977: 233; quoting Husserl, 1931: 96)

In other words by resting the meanings of the social world entirely on what Schutz calls the typifications of consciousness, phenomenology ignores influences on social life that exist beyond consciousness.

I agree with Bourdieu's criticism of phenomenology; the problem is that he does not fully justify his criticism. Although phenomenology seeks a return "to the things themselves" through a reflective grasp of the world of "primary experience," it misses the *sociohistorical texture of "primary experience"* by failing to escape the very theoretical bifurcation of subject and world that it revolts against. A recovery of the "essential structure" of experience is intertwined with consideration of the "economic and social conditions" of everyday life. The failure of phenomenology—or, more specifically, of the phenomenological perspective that has held the most currency within sociology—to shake free of certain presuppositions prevents such a recovery.

Suspending the presupposition of a split between subject and world forces us to reject the reduction of the problem of experience to processes and typifications of intentional constitution. Bourdieu accepts this reduction implicitly in his dismissal of an analytical focus on experience. When experience is seen to be irreducible to intentional constitution, phenomenological reflection need no longer be considered incompatible with a sociological interest in historically developed conditions of human existence. I contend that exploring prereflective experience is essential to disclosing the power of habitus within everyday life.[3] More specifically, such disclosure is accomplished by grounding the sociohistorical phenomenon of habitus within the dynamics of intersubjective sensitivity. I hope to demonstrate this in an analysis of elementary school classroom experience as it is comprehensible in terms of the social position of being a pupil.

The theory of habitus

In his early philosophical writings Marx attacks the perspectives of both objective determinism and subjective idealism for their failure to grasp the generative conditions of social reality. Marx rejects idealist philosophy for its blindness to the historical-material foundations of human consciousness, but he also repudiates "all hitherto existing materialism—that of Feuerbach included" for its reduction of reality to the status of an "object or of *contemplation.*" Explicating social reality "subjectively"—as "human sensuous activity" (Marx, 1947: 197)—is as fundamental to the conception of materialist philosophy developed in Marx's early writings as the discovery of the dialectic between social relations and means of production that underlies the history of ideas and practices. The problem is to grasp *how* the "superstructure" of human reality—the everyday world of thought, values, and beliefs—manifests the "substructure," the historically developed social relations of production, which have their most concrete expression in the divisions between the owning and working classes.

Yet Marx never seriously explores how "substructure" is fundamental to the structure of experience. In fact, he virtually abandons the problem of "human sensuous activity" in his later writings, where the theoretical objective becomes the demonstration of a causal relationship between substructure and superstructure through empirical studies of the historically variable socioeconomic system. Pierre Bourdieu's work is devoted to reviving and elaborating on the problem of social reality as a *manifestation* of historically and, in that sense, "objectively" given social relationships.

There is nothing particularly novel about such an analytical task; indeed, it is the point of departure for Mannheim's development of the "sociology of knowledge." What distinguishes Bourdieu's approach is his theory of habitus, which represents an alternative to the view that the dialectic of social position and consciousness is essentially a matter of accumulating knowledge—whether explicit or taken-for-granted. Bourdieu seeks to explicate the sociohistorical foundation of human reality in terms of the " 'visceral' tastes and distastes" (Bourdieu, 1984: 475) of the habitual body.[4] There is thus the interesting sociological paradox that the human body, which is "commonly perceived as the most natural expression of innermost nature" (Bourdieu, 1984: 192), is in fact an *embodiment* of such "objectively given" positions as one's age, gender, race, or class in the social environment.[5]

With the concept of "taste," which carries the double meaning of the disposition to "perceive flavors" and to "discern aesthetic values" (Bourdieu, 1984: 474), Bourdieu means to disclose this embodiment without reducing it to a mechanical response to "outside forces." In opposition to economic determinism Bourdieu emphasizes that a life-style centered in economic necessity is no less a fulfillment of acquired tastes than one characterized by the absence of necessity (Bourdieu, 1984).[6] When Marx asserts that "the division of labor brands the manufacturing laborer as the property of capital," the "brand" is precisely a matter of habitus, comprised of *tastes* "for what [one is] anyway condemned to" (Bourdieu, 1984: 178-179).

We inhabit environments of limits and options that are demarcated "objectively" by our being either male or female, young or old, patient or doctor, student or teacher, working class or professional, white or black. It is by virtue of our dispositions formed within these limits and options that our "sense of reality" is conditioned by our social positions. These dispositions are habitual reminders of the distance between social positions as well as

> the conduct required in order to "keep one's distance" or to manipulate it strategically, whether symbolically or actually, to reduce it (easier for the dominant than for the dominated), increase it, or simply maintain it (by not "letting oneself go," not "becoming familiar," in short, "standing on one's dignity," or on the other hand, refusing to "take liberties" and "put oneself forward," in short, "knowing one's place" and staying there). (Bourdieu, 1977: 82)

"Knowing one's place" is a habitual separation of self "from the goods, persons, places, and so forth from which one is excluded [i.e., excluded 'objectively']" (Bourdieu, 1984: 471). Bourdieu emphasizes that this *sense* of one's limits is also a blindness to their existence (Bourdieu, 1984: 471). Stated differently, the socio-logical limits of social position are typically "misrecognized," which is to say, they appear as "natural" possibilities of self, embodied, for instance, in the expression, "That's not for the likes of us." The notion of misrecognition is at the heart of Bourdieu's claim that through habitus the social order is *reproduced* as if it were the "natural" perpetuation of conditions for which, viewed from the standpoint of our "place" within them, we were "naturally made." The theory of habitus is intended to demonstrate that we "re-produce" in our "verdict on [ourselves] the verdict the economy pronounces on [us]" (Bourdieu, 1984: 471).

In a paper entitled "Men and Machines" (Bourdieu, 1981) Bourdieu applies the theory of habitus to a critique of Sartre's famous description of the café waiter. Sartre contends that the café waiter "plays with his condition in order to *realize* it" (Sartre, 1956: 102). Waitering is, for Sartre, a performance that, in the last analysis, one has the freedom to either choose or refuse. In that sense one cannot *be* a waiter,

> which means that I can be he only in *representation*. But if I represent myself as him, I am not he; I am separated from him as the object from the subject, separated by *nothing*, but this nothing isolates me from him. I cannot be he, I can only play *at being* him; that is, imagine to myself that I am he. (Sartre, 1956: 102-103)

Bourdieu contends that Sartre fails to see that being a waiter is more than playing a role; it is a submersion within the socio-historical conditions in which one embodies the dispositions of a waiter. Thus, against Sartre, Bourdieu argues that the waiter:

> cannot even be said to take himself for a café waiter; he is too much taken up in the job which was naturally (i.e., socio-logically) assigned to him (e.g., as the son of a shopkeeper who needs to earn enough to set up his own business) even to have the idea of such role-distance. By contrast, one only has to put a student in his position...to see him manifesting in countless ways the aloofness he intends to maintain, precisely by affecting to perform it as a *role, vis-à-vis* a job which he does not feel "made" for. (Bourdieu, 1981: 309)

The student with upper-middle-class roots, no less than the working-class son of a shopkeeper, embodies a certain habitus that shapes how he inhabits and how he identifies with the inhabitation of particular institutional contexts of practice (e.g., workplace, school, family). There is also the habitus of the "intellectual" who "distances himself no more than the waiter from his own position and from what specifically defines it, i.e., the illusion of distance from all positions" (Bourdieu, 1981: 310). Bourdieu argues that this illusion is exemplified by Sartre's characterization of the waiter. Sartre "projects an intellectual's consciousness into a café waiter's practice,"

> producing a sort of social chimera, a monster with a waiter's body and a philosopher's head. One surely has to have the freedom to stay in bed *without* being fired in order to find that someone who gets up at five to sweep the café...is (freely?) freeing himself from the freedom to stay in bed even if it means being fired. (Bourdieu, 1981: 310)

Acquired habit is, for Sartre, an obstruction to *choice*, or rather, it is a form of "bad faith," which is the denial of one's own freedom to choose. I have already noted Sartre's failure to recognize that preobjective habit is an experiential precondition of conscious choice (cf. Chapter 2). Bourdieu is, however, no more interested than Sartre in formulating such a precondition. Bourdieu argues that habitus is a "practical comprehension" of the world that typically dispenses with the need to "constitute" its meanings in consciousness. He contends that a phenomenological return to experience remains inherently blind to the sociological conditions of inhabiting the world because it ignores this sociohistorical "obviation" of intentionality by habitus (Bourdieu, 1977). Yet here Bourdieu commits the same error as that of the phenomenologists he opposes: He conflates the phenomena of experience and consciousness. With his aversion to phenomenological reflection Bourdieu misses the deeper implications of his rejection of Sartre's account of the café waiter: Sartre's sociological blindness is also a phenomenological blindness to the habitual grounds of consciousness. That is, Sartre fails to see that a preobjective sensitivity to a world demarcated by one's social position is foundational to the very *possibility* of consciousness.

Institutional inhabitation: The case of the classroom

Nowhere is the necessity of grounding habitus in the structure of immediate experience more apparent than in Bourdieu's own opposition to a "mechanistic" view of conformity within such bureaucratic institutions as public schools or factories. Bourdieu claims that even within the most "totalitarian institutions"[7]

> analysis reveals a sort of unconscious adjustment of positions and dispositions, the true principle of the functioning of the institution, precisely in the aspect which gives it the appearance of an infernal machine. (Bourdieu, 1981: 314)

The "unconscious adjustment of positions and dispositions" creates what Bourdieu calls a "tacit agreement" between institutional conditions of practice and the inhabitants of institutions (Bourdieu, 1981: 314). This is essentially the point that he makes in his study with Passeron of the role of the educational system in the legitimization and reproduction of class hierarchy in industrial society. Here he contends that "pedagogic work" must be understood as a simultaneous production of material and symbolic *objects* of interest and dersire and of the *propensity* to be interested in and desire them. Otherwise,

> one is condemned to interminable speculation as to the priority of the veneration or the venerable, the adoration or the adorable, the respect or the respectable, the admiration or the admirable, etc., that is, to oscillate between trying to deduce the dispositions toward the object from the intrinsic properties of the object and trying to reduce the properties conferred on it by the dispositions of the subject. (Bourdieu and Passeron, 1977: 39)

Bourdieu means to demonstrate that although, as he claims in his criticism of both Sartre and the "interactionist" or "psychosocial" perspectives in sociology, conformity is not typically reducible to "strategies" or intellectual "choices," neither do we conform, following the "structuralist view," out of a blind response to the "iron laws" of bureaucracies, as if we were machines. Rather, the dispositions acquired from the time of childhood render certain environments sensible, and we develop a sense for what is "reinforced" by our experiences within them (Bourdieu, 1981).

Yet until the "tacit agreement" between institutions and individuals is grounded in the "thickness of the preobjective present" (Merleau-Ponty, 1962: 433), the notions of habitus and, in fact, social position remain no less theoretically detached from everyday life than either the "iron laws" of structuralist theory or the free-floating chimera that Sartre makes of the waiter's consciousness. For instance, saying that "pedagogic work" produces either objects of disposition or dispositions toward objects already circumvents the *preobjective* structure of the pupil's sensitivity to classroom life. We need to explore the environment as it is *instituted*, prior to the constitutive activity of consciousness, within social conditions of experience. Through this exploration we can delineate what could be called the lived texture of social position—the prereflective experience of inhabiting a sociohistorically demarcated "place" within the social environment.

I have chosen to focus on the pupil's place within the world of the classroom in order to explicate social position as a preobjective context of experience. In his study of education Bourdieu is at pains to point out that the power of the educational system to help reproduce the social hierarchy of class relations is owed largely to its relative institutional autonomy. When sociology has focused on this reproduction, it has tended to ignore the peculiar workings of the educational system *as such*, in favor of viewing it as a simple "reflection" of class structure. Bourdieu contends that this form of analysis bypasses the "differential function" of the educational system in relation to class structure, or, more specifically, its simultaneous social function of "reproducing class relations, by ensuring the hereditary transmission of cultural capital, and its ideological function of concealing that social function by accrediting the illusion of its absolute autonomy" (Bourdieu and Passeron, 1977: 191, 199). Yet although Bourdieu wants to capture the specific role that educational institutions play in what he calls the "inculcation" of social dispositions, he attends less to social positions *within* the classroom than those outside of it. In this way he misses how experiential preconditions of the school system's legitimization of social order are located in the dynamics of *being a pupil* in the classroom.

The pupil's social position *as pupil* is comprehensible as a constantly shifting placement within a field of possibilities for behavior and expression. The following analysis of one moment of classroom life focuses on how shifts in each pupil's practical mobility both immerse pupils in the intersubjectivity of "their class" and provide for their sense of "failure" or "success" vis-à-vis one another. The *institutional position* that binds pupils together is the context for their experiences of varying *classroom positions*. By locating the underlying sensitivity of these experiences, we also discover what could be called the habitual pretext for the "academic consecration" (Bourdieu and Passeron, 1977: xii) of social inequities of power and privilege.

During a question and answer session in a conventional classroom setting, a pupil stands before his class at the blackboard:[8]

Boris had trouble reducing "12/16" to the lowest terms, and could only get as far as "6/8." The teacher asked him quietly if that was as far as he could reduce it. She suggested he "think." Much heaving up and down and waving of hands by other children, all frantic to correct him. Boris, pretty unhappy, probably mentally paralyzed. The teacher, quiet, patient, ignores the others and concentrates with look and voice on Boris. She says, "Is there a bigger number than two you can divide into the two parts of the fraction?" After a minute or two, she becomes more urgent, but there is no response from Boris. She then turns to the class and says, "Well, who can tell Boris what the number is?" A forest of hands appears, and the teacher calls Peggy. Peggy says that four may be divided into the numerator and the denominator. (Henry, 1963: 295-296)

"Pedagogic work" certainly delimits pupils' possibilities of experience in the classroom that is described in this example. The teacher solicits pupils to be visibly productive in the styles of expression that she prescribes for each lesson. These pedagogic solicitations and prescriptions are regular occurrences for pupils and, thus, rarely matters for reflection. Beyond their "taken-for-granted" status in reflection, however, the pedagogic conditions of classroom life are vivid in experience—intense enough to occasion a variety of emotions, including unhappiness, yearning, or joy. Boris' unhappiness seems "only natural" to anyone familiar with the conventional classroom setting: How else does one experience such failure—especially failure in the eyes of so many? Yet how do "failure" or "success" exist as possibilities that are instituted as contexts of experience?

Boris fails to "think," meaning that he cannot fill the teacher's prescription for expression at this moment at the blackboard. He is caught in limbo between the building intensity of his "mental paralysis" and the solicitations for expression that he is unable to engage. Yet his productive inertia is not his alone, as if this event occurred solely "within his consciousness," outside of the ebb and flow, or *tempo,*[9] of classroom activity. It is precisely the individual's *visibility* before the class that provides for his or her force of presence in the classroom. This is not to say that the pupil becomes simply an object of attention—a mere spectacle for the group. By being singularly visible in the classroom, the pupil has a preobjective, corporeal impact on the practical tempo that binds teacher and pupils *as a group*, steeping them within the inter-corporeal rhythm of classroom life.

As he stands frozen at the pedagogic locus of the classroom, Boris simultaneously freezes the "classroom tempo": The productive rhythm of the class is brought to its heels by his very existence at the blackboard. The teacher in fact institutes and sustains a productive lapse by holding Boris in place, as it were, refusing to acknowledge the flurry of hands behind them. His expressive paralysis thereby endures within an institutional setting as a fundamentally *intersubjective* phenomenon. Through a reflexive sensitivity to his impact within the intersubjectivity of classroom life Boris has a *sense of failure* that is peculiar to the habitus of the pupil in the compulsory school classroom.

The same kind of sensitivity lies at the heart of a pupil's sense of success. The pupils who raise their hands anticipate an opportunity to inhabit the productive space that will become "free" following Boris' release. Yet the setting for this anticipation is a volatile one: The status of each pupil's chances shifts with each moment that the teacher delays her abandonment of Boris. For instance, the early handraiser, whose visibility diminishes with growing numbers of raised hands, suffers a progressive weakening of his or her opportunities. There exists the irony that the very activity that provides pupils with some power of determination over the focus of pedagogic attention also perpetuates their powerlessness with regard to it. Handraising is thus one way that pupils help to *reproduce* their social position within this institution.

When the teacher turns toward the class and asks "Well, who can tell Boris what the number is?", Boris' failure is objectified for the group, and this neutralizes the force of his presence *within* the group. While the teacher may appear to be soliciting pedagogical assistance on Boris' behalf, it is surely his displacement from the productive space of the classroom that matters for the rest of the class as their handraising intensifies. Similarly, while Peggy's "success" is obviously *known* by her and anyone else to be located in the "correctness" of her response, her *sense* of success is grounded in a sensitivity to the spatiotemporal status of her presence in the classroom. When she is chosen to speak, she appropriates the productive intensity of the area in which Boris still stands—virtually draws it to herself, its locus reemerging at her desk. Remaining in "her place," Peggy thereby emerges out of the shared uncertainty as to "where one stands" that is specific to the pupil's social position.

The temporary transformation of Peggy's practical posture is earned only at the expense of those around her who strive for the same. Here is a fiercely competitive situation that would horrify members of many nonindustrial cultures (Henry, 1963: 296). Yet this is not competition "for its own sake," or a matter of "transmitted values" somehow absorbed by and then governing the behavior of pupils, as if they were machines. The "competitiveness" among pupils is rooted to the context in which a teacher exercises her power over their practical mobility vis-á-vis one another. Their competitiveness is, in short, part of the more general phenomenon of the practical perspective, or habitus, which is comprised of the sensitivity that steeps pupils within the intersubjectivity of classroom life.

To be a pupil is to be sensitive to the shifting spatial loci and fluctuating temporal rhythms of that singular institutional contact that one knows simply as "the class." This suggests more than a "tacit agreement" or "doxic relationship" (Bourdieu, 1977) between individual and institution. As "taken-for-granted" as the spatiotemporal metamorphoses of classroom life may be in *reflection*, prior to reflection they are dramatic: They recast, sometimes in abrupt and shocking ways (as when the teacher catches someone "goofing off"), the focus of pedagogic attention and, correspondingly, the intensity of any one pupil's luminosity within the classroom.

The sensitivity of pupils to the intricacies of this drama is also a sensitivity to their practical distances from one another—indeed, to an environment of disparate social power and privileges. This environment seems "only natural," which is to say, it provides for, as a matter of habit, pupils' very freedom to anticipate, choose, and even create possibilities for inhabiting the classroom. Privileges, however, are conferred upon and *recur for* only those who attain them through the work that is pedagogically consecrated as scholastic achievement. Pupils are thus free to be exactly who they are from the vantage points of *what they are* within the historically specific conditions of social hierarchy in the classroom. If, as Bourdieu and others show,[10] compulsory schooling reproduces the inequities of the broader social structure, a habitual pretext of this reproduction is to be found in the pupil's sensitivity to his institutionally pregiven social position *as a pupil* in the classroom and the shifting order of power and privilege that is intrinsic to it.

The embodiment of social position

The "conditioned and conditional freedom" that is secured by habits of involvement in the compulsory school classroom, or any social setting, is "as remote from a creation of unpredictable novelty as it is from a simple mechanical reproduction of the initial conditioning" (Bourdieu, 1977: 95). We are not merely involved "in the environment," however, as if we were nothing more than relatively competent visitors on the scene. We inhabit *situations*, the qualities and intensities of which, the very existence of which, are inseparable from our immersion within them. When habit is understood as the preobjective *sensitivity* to these situations, it is possible to penetrate into the interior of both the world that is freed up by its acquisition and the "reproduction" of social positions in this world.

Yet along with this analytical penetration into prereflective experience comes the realization that social position can no longer be taken to be an "objective phenomenon," as though it were a "thing" functioning independently of human experience. We can, to use Dewey's term, "denote" the phenomenon as a persistent force in the present, but its *forcefulness* is not "objectively" determined, and so it cannot be demarcated with "objective certainty." The power of "a social position" is indeterminate experientially and, therefore, ambiguous analytically. Economic class, age, gender, race, and any other positions that can be pointed to are not separate, objective realms of human life, or rather they are distinguished only through their representations in reflection. In experience various positions in the social world coalesce as converging and shifting forces of sensitivity in our situations.

"The problem of the world, and to begin with, that of one's own body, consists in the fact that it *is all there*" (Merleau-Ponty, 1962: 198). We are as entangled preobjectively with "the outside world" as with our own bodies, and this double entanglement lies at the phenomenological heart of the structure of social position. Bourdieu observes that in French culture being female and male are contrasting forms of corporeal habitus: Talking from the front of one's mouth as opposed to with the whole mouth—especially from the back of the mouth and the throat; blowing the nose with a kleenex, with its soft, delicate texture, as opposed to hard and loud with a big cotton handkerchief, "with the eyes closed and the nose held tightly"; laughing in a constricted, "repressed" way as opposed to a "belly laugh, with wrinkled nose, wide-open mouth and deep breathing" (Bourdieu, 1984: 191). These are distinctions between the male and female bodies' styles of movement and expression; but what of the world that "is all there" through these habitual styles? If bellowing, heaving laughter, a delicately hushed sneeze, or a pupil's forward-bending, back-arching, outstretched handwaving seem "only natural" during their engagement, it is because we find ourselves in fresh situations *through* our corporeal inherence in the environment. The ways of the body are not reducible to "practices"; they are the media of the sense of our situations, which is to say, they embody sensitivity to the world.

The preobjective complexity of being-in-a-situation compels us to reject the notion of an objectively discernible "path" from social position to action (including what Bourdieu calls "improvised" action). I carry social positions within me.[11] I belong to them by virtue of their belonging to me as part of the deeply personal fabric of my being-in-the-world. They are, in short, contexts of habit, but not merely in Bourdieu's sense of habitus as the manifestation in practice of impersonal forces that impinge upon my existence. Bourdieu misses the way that prereflective presence is permeated and contextualized, and only thereby *controlled* by habituation. Whatever social positions amount to for persons is strictly a matter of experience, where prior to positing objects of reflection we are sensitive to an inherently social world and to our limits and freedoms within it.

Habit and possibility

In Bernard Malamud's *The Fixer* Yakov Bok asks "Why me?" as he awaits execution for a crime that it is not even within him to commit. It is, he thinks, "his various shortcomings and mistakes" that plunge him into an "endless series of miserable events." Yet it is more than that; his predicament is owed not only to his individual characteristics but to "force of circumstance," being a Jew in Tsarist Russia, "though how you separated one from the other—if one really could—was beyond him" (Malamud, 1966: 281).

Our situations are saturated with the "force of circumstance" that submerges us within them, and so who we are is inseparable from what we are in the social world. How do I sort out this matrix of positions that are at once my historicity and my "thrownness" into the present (Heidegger, 1962)? I am a white, Jewish, suburban-bred son of a lawyer, a man, a husband, a father, a teacher, a colleague—I am all of these things at once. Yet these are not mere things; they are fused through the "cohesion without concept" that is also the preobjective coherence—the *sense*—of my world.

I feel the weight of my obligations to others, which are the obligations to myself—a habitual self that is at once sensitive to an inescapably intersubjective world. I push hard to complete this analytical project, thrilling myself as I reach the completion points that are also consummations of who I am for others, "making me whole within a 'we'" (Ricoeur, 1966: 128). I am also drawn, for the same socio-logical reasons, by the pull of the restfulness of disengagement, which is precisely the pull of the "homelife" that I am sensitive to (without the necessity of any specific awareness of my "positions" as husband or father), within the knot of sociality that constitutes it. I feel the weight of various dimensions of my intersubjective habituality as they converge on my sense of what I am doing and of myself doing it.

Are we locked, then, into behaviors and decisions that are determined by social pressures to which we are condemned by the mere fact of our historical existence? We are condemned to these pressures, but they do not determine us, as their force comes only in and through the situations that we confront anew in every experience. These pressures wax and wane, fade in and out, in their impact on the qualities and intensities of situations. It can happen that certain social positions from which we have not escaped recede for a time, their habitual force diminished, if never entirely extinguished, as contexts of possibility and constraint. We may even still have contact with those with whom such social positions were established as media of sensitivity, the significance of certain aspects of our copresence becoming dull in the wake of others. There is also the possibility of the emergence of new positions, or the resurgence of old ones, in the preobjective constitution of our situations.

The habitual grounds of our social being are, to varying degrees, in flux. We are steeped in the recession, the resurgence, the emergence of the very sensitivity that roots us to the dialectic between "objectively given" and personal history. An absence of *absolute* freedom establishes, in other words, the "atmosphere of freedom" that characterizes human existence (Merleau-Ponty, 1962). This is not to refer merely to Bourdieu's "conditioned and conditional freedom." We may become what we once were or what we have not yet been. New projects are always possible, as are qualitative shifts in those that already engage us. It is by being situated historically through our own habituation that we are empowered to *know* our existence and, perhaps, to free ourselves from what we are in the present.

> He had learned, it wasn't easy; the experience was his; it was worse than that, it was he. He was the experience. It also meant that now he was somebody else than he had been, who would have thought it? So I learned a little, he thought, I learned this but what good will it do me? Will it open the prison doors? Will it allow me to go out and take up my poor life again? Will it free me a little once I am free? Or have I only learned to know what my condition is—that the ocean is salty as you are drowning, and though you knew it you are drowned? Still, it was better than not knowing. A man had to learn, it was his nature. (Malamud, 1966: 283)

The possibilities that inhere in this knowledge, because its source is the thinker's habitual entanglement with the world, extend beyond knowledge:

Nothing determines me from outside, not because nothing acts upon me, but, on the contrary, because I am from the start outside myself and open to the world. We are *true* through and through, and have with us, by the mere fact of belonging to the world, and not merely being in the world in the way that things are, all that we need to transcend ourselves. (Merleau-Ponty, 1962: 456)

Chapter Six

Conclusion:
Sociology and Human Experience

Through habits formed in intercourse with the world, we also inhabit the world. It becomes a home and the home is a part of our every experience.

John Dewey
Art as Experience

The "home" of which Dewey speaks is the experiential antecedent to positing a separation between subject and world. When this antecedent itself becomes the object of thematization, reflection reaches toward the conditions that determine the possibility of reflection. Dewey names this process of exploring the back side of the very activity in which I am engaged the "denotative" method of philosophy (Dewey, 1929). Merleau-Ponty simply calls it "true reflection":

True reflection presents me to myself not as idle and inaccessible subjectivity, but as identical with my presence in the world and to others, as I am now realizing it: I am all that I see, I am an intersubjective field, not despite my body and historical situation, but, on the contrary, by being this body and this situation, and through them, all the rest. (Merleau-Ponty, 1962: 452)

When Merleau-Ponty says that I am "identical with my presence in the world," he discloses a fundamental paradox of phenomenological reflection: In order to construe the world as I live it I must in effect deny the conceptual discriminations that comprise the construction. As Dewey shows, saying that the habitual entanglement of self and world can be reduced to a "composite" by analytical measures is not the same as saying that it exists as a composite prior to the exercise of these measures (cf. Chapter 1). The distinction between self and world that provides the logic of the formulation is an artifact of reflection; it is not intrinsic to what is *pointed to* by the formulation. "True reflection" is reflection that remains obsessed with its own limitations, remaining true to experience by avoiding the error of formulating its structure as if it were ordered by the logical apparatus of the formulation.

It is as "true reflection" that phenomenological philosophy can supply sociology with a "vigilance which does not let us forget the source of all knowledge" (Merleau-Ponty, 1964b: 110). Yet the "prejudice of determinate being" persists throughout the social sciences as a powerful predisposition to such forgetfulness, with reflection butting up against a world that seems to be an infinitely reducible composite of objects of thematized or taken-for-granted knowledge. This prejudice is more than a blindness to the experiential foundation of knowledge: It operates as a methodological principle that rules out the *validity* of claims that are not documented in terms of "empirical evidence," which is to say, in terms of objects of verifiable observations. The purely nonreflective, qualitative immediacy of the world is thus eliminated from analytical consideration by virtue of its preobjective status in experience.[1]

The prejudice of determinate being amounts to a methodological constraint that effectively severs the connection between theoretical explication and the *implicit* character of inhabiting the world. When we break free of this constraint it becomes possible to "lift out" as explicit qualities of experience what are already "there" for us, but not noticed and discriminated as such (Gendlin, 1973). In this methodological light consider the example from Balázs' *Theory of Film* that was cited in Chapter 3:

> The hero of the film is a Chinese merchant. Lillian Gish, playing a beggar-girl who is being pursued by enemies, collapses at his door. The Chinese merchant finds her, carries her into his house and looks after the sick girl. The girl slowly recovers, but her face remains stone-like in its sorrow. "Can't you smile?" the Chinese asks the frightened child who is only just beginning to trust him. "I'll try," says Lillian Gish, picks up a mirror and goes through the motions of a smile, aiding her face muscles with her fingers. The result is a painful, even horrible mask which the girl now turns toward the Chinese merchant. But his

kindly friendly eyes bring a real smile to her face. The face does not change; but a warm emotion lights it up from inside and an intangible nuance turns the grimace into a real expression. (Balász, 1979: 295)

I suggest that we contend theoretically with the evocative power of this description at precisely the level of consideration that is ruled out by adherence to the predominant methodological constraints of the social sciences. The passage describes two facial expressions that are apparently indistinguishable in their explicit, or "objective," features. Yet from the characters' standpoints these expressions are profoundly different from one another, and the description *signifies* how this is so. This is not to say that the difference is understood by the reader as a matter of signification, as if the characters distinguished the two smiles *conceptually*. Rather, the description employs metaphors that "enable us to think, that is, to have traffic with" (Arendt, 1971: 110) the *sense* that antecedes signification. At the level of its nonreflective sense the "intangible nuance" that "turns the grimace into a real expression" is not demonstrable in an empirically verifiable way, but these metaphors are plausible as references to the qualitative immediacy of gestures within their lived social context. The *implicit* transformation of Gish's expression embodies the "immediate and immanent meaning" of her and the merchant's intersubjective contact; that is how it *matters* experientially, as experience is reflected in Balázs' description.

In addition to reading Balázs' account of the scene we may, of course, view it for ourselves. Recognizing the transformation that Balázs describes is, in either case, hardly contingent upon the "truth" of what individuals are actually undergoing, which may have more to do with actors attending to a script and camera crew than "real feeling." In discussions of film or literature the irrelevance of empirical truth is sometimes referred to as the "suspension of disbelief." The idea is that the plausibility of depicted situations requires the viewer or reader to ignore the issue of their "reality" for "real persons." This idea is, no doubt, true enough, but we may comprehend the plausibility of description in more positive terms: The "lived" intensities of "characters' " expressions and, for that matter, the expressions of the "subjects" of sociological observation are as perceivable as the expressions of those with whom we interact. Our intersubjective sensitivity predisposes us to perceive, if not "prove" that we perceive, the prereflective experience of social situations, which is thereby available for description.

Explicating immediate experience is not, therefore, a matter of claiming access to the "actual content" of anyone's experiences. We must put aside certain empirical restrictions on the possibilities of observation and description and, to use Kurt H. Wolff's term, "surrender" to our essential predisposition to *see* beyond the physical or conceptual characteristics of human involvement in a social world. It is in this way that an analytical "catch" of the prereflective texture of social life is possible (Wolff, 1976). The *validity* of what is caught is not contingent on its demonstrable "accuracy" for particular individuals, but on the evocative power of the argument—evocative insofar as readers are pointed to their own immersion in the world in a way that renders explicit the otherwise implicit structure of this immersion.

In *Sociology as an Art Form* Robert Nisbet writes of the "intellectual drouth and barrenness" that results from the tendency in sociology to make the act of analytical discovery conform to the rules and prescriptions that comprise the logic of empirical demonstration (1976: 5). Imagine, Nisbet observes, if Marx, Weber, Durkheim, or Simmel had subjugated their inquiries to

> demonstrating solely what had been arrived at through aseptic problem design, through meticulous verification, and through constructions of theory which would pass muster in a graduate course in methodology of sociology today...the entire world of thought would be much poorer. (1976: 7)

Nisbet is not suggesting that creative scholarship rely upon a theoretical detachment from the concrete world; on the contrary, he reveals that insight into the constitution of this world may be smothered by methodological rules that filter out possibilities of its visibility to reflection. Nisbet's thesis of the "crucial difference" between the logical requirements of discovery and demonstration can be restated as follows: The logic of discovery *is* intertwined with the logic of demonstration, but criteria for demonstration must be invented in terms of the aims of discovery.[2] We then recover a world that is open to theoretical illumination.

Interpretive sociology aims to illuminate the social world from its lived, or "subjective," standpoint. Yet in order to raise the experiential depth of social situations to the level of explication we must violate principles of demonstration that appear inviolate within the discipline. New criteria need to be established for rendering the world visible to reflection. The alternative is to confuse the subject's reality with the composite of objects that reflection makes of it. We then continue to project into the world our theoretical relationship to it, or commit the fallacy of which Marx accused Hegel: taking the "things of logic for the logic of things" (Bourdieu, 1981: 305). This fallacy compromises the effort of interpretive sociology to acquire an "unreflected sensitivity" to the lived meanings of the social world (Winch, 1958).[3] It will remain until we crack through the "prejudice of determinate being" that sustains it.[4]

The writings of Merleau-Ponty and Dewey stand out within twentieth-century philosophy for their consistent opposition to this prejudice. There is perhaps no better evidence of its persistence within sociology than each writer's neglect within the discipline. Merleau-Ponty's legacy is, for the most part, confined to scattered acknowledgments of the significance of "the body." His refocusing of phenomenology on the "antepredicative unity of the world and our life" (Merleau-Ponty, 1962: 61) has been overshadowed by Schutz's more explicit discussions of phenomenological sociology. It could be argued that Dewey's emphasis on the embeddedness of the workings of mind within possibilities of interaction between self and environment was a central impetus behind the focus on social interaction in American sociology. Nevertheless, Mead's identification of American pragmatism with problems of behavioral and conceptual adaptations to the environment have all but obviated the relevance of Dewey's "denotative" philosophy of the qualitative immediacy of the world for contemporary sociologists.

The philosophical perspectives of both Merleau-Ponty and Dewey point to a precedent within the structure of immediate experience for discriminating human existence sociologically. That precedent is the habitual sensitivity that is essential to inhabiting a world that matters in its immediate sense and will continue to be made sense of. Dewey refers to habit as the "banks" of the stream of ideas and feelings: There can be no consciousness *of* the world apart from a preobjective, habitual infusion of self *within* the world (Dewey, 1925:8). It is precisely at the point of this infusion that we are entrenched within social relationships. We are part of one another's experience in a more fundamental way than being objects to either our own or others' consciousness. Indeed, our sensitivity to the existence of others lies at the banks of experience as an underlying condition of consciousness.

Phenomenological reflection provides a philosophical foundation for sociology by establishing the primordial interwovenness of human subject and social world. This is not to be confused with the relationship between phenomenology and sociological analysis that is articulated by Schutz. He argues that at its transcendental-philosophical level phenomenology cannot *in itself* elucidate social aspects of human existence. What is sought is the sphere of pure consciousness that lies beneath all constituted features of the everyday world, including anything that could be called social. This reduction makes it possible to delineate the fundamental principles of intentional constitution that can be applied *subsequently* to sociological analyses of the *constituted* structure of social reality. Phenomenological philosophy thereby supplies a conceptual "first step" to describing the social structure of everyday life.

I am suggesting a more substantive role for phenomenological philosophy in the discipline of sociology. Elaborating on what he takes to be Husserl's move away from the notion of a pure, constituting consciousness to a concern with the "life-world," Merleau-Ponty argues that our relationship to the environment is no more reducible to intentionality than the experience of our own bodies. The problem of "transcendental subjectivity" is not one of an "ego" posed beneath and constituting the meanings of the world or one's place within it, and social reality is not a consequence of meaning-constitution, Schutz's notion of such meaning being "typified" notwithstanding. I am bound preobjectively with the environment and, thus, can no longer be conceived in isolation of my social conditions—whether as their interpretive creator or "objective" consequence. I am at the outset steeped within a dialectic between habitual sensitivity and sociohistorical contexts of inhabitation. Moving beyond Schutz, phenomenological philosophy offers more than a conceptual precursor to a theory of social life: Sociology has its concrete beginnings in the exposure of the sociality of human existence at the "back side of things that we have not constituted" (Merleau-Ponty, 1964b: 180), at the essential core of human experience.

NOTES

1. Dilthey's formulation of the proper subject matter of the *Geisteswissenschaften* (translatable as "human studies") is based on a conception of experience that is similar to Husserl's; in fact, Dilthey virtually invented the term *Erlebnis* (typically translated as "lived" or "immediate" experience) as a singular noun for German philosophy. Dilthey writes: "The way in which lived experience presents itself to me [literally, 'is-there-for-me'] is completely different from the way in which images stand before me. The consciousness of the experience and its constitution are the same; there is no separation between what is there-for-me and what *in* experience is there-for-me. In other words, experience does not stand like an object over against the experiencer, but rather its very existence for me is undifferentiated from the *whatness* which is present for me in it" (Dilthey, 1958: 139; passage translated by Palmer, 1969: 109).

Dilthey argues that *Verstehen*, as a method of human study, is the effort to understand this lived experience. He contends that it is possible to achieve such understanding by virtue of the fact that the lived depth of experience, which he describes as an "inner state," objectifies itself in "expressions of life" (Dilthey [excerpts] in Truzzi, 1974: 16-17).

2. See the edited collection by Truzzi, 1974, for several excellent treatments of this distinction. The text includes a discussion of and excerpts from Dilthey's arguments on the "special character" of the human sciences.

3. Weber's principal statements on *Verstehen* as a sociological method appear in *The Theory of Social and Economic Organization* (1947) and *The Methodology of the Social Sciences* (1949).

Weber writes: "The means employed by the method of 'understanding explanation' are not *normative* correctness, but rather, on the one hand, the concentrated habits of the investigator and teacher in thinking in a particular way, and on the other, as the situation requires, his capacity to 'feel himself' *empathically into a mode of thought* which deviates from his own and which is normatively 'false' according to his own habits of thought" (Weber, 1949: 41).

Winch develops Weber's opposition of the problems of the social sciences versus the natural sciences in *The Idea of a Social Science* (1958). Winch argues that the social scientist is always confronted with two social contexts of "rules"—that of his own practical involvement as a social scientist, with his priorities of what "counts as subject matter," and those of the people he studies. The natural scientist has no such problem; he only deals in *one* social context—his own. The sociologist who explains human behavior in statistical or any other so-called "objective" terms has removed himself from the possibility of *Verstehen*—grasping and elucidating the structure of behavior as it has *meaning* for its subjects.

For example, Vilfredo Pareto looks at all action from the perspective of scientific logic and on this basis differentiates logical and nonlogical behavior. In this way he misses that any "logic" is "only intelligible in the context of ways of living or modes of social life" (Winch, 1958: 100). Pareto argues that Christian rites of baptism share the same "residual factor" as the actions of a pagan "sprinkling lustral water or letting sacrificial blood" (Winch, 1958: 108), meaning they have the same invariant factor of the use of liquid in the service of some kind of "purification." Winch counters that a Christian or pagan would deny such a connection, precisely because of the profound differences in the ways of living that give the rites their logical sense (or, in Weber's terms, give them their "intended meanings"). This ground of the ritual's sense, the point that it has within a social context, is the fundamental *sociological* issue, and it is exactly what Pareto excludes from consideration.

Winch contends that Durkheim makes a similar mistake in defining "suicide" apart from the contextually specific sense of the concept of suicide in the various societies mentioned in his famous study. In Winch's view, by defining the concept in an objectively generalizable way, Durkheim has already removed himself from the possibility of understanding suicide sociologically—according to its contextually relative logic.

4. Winch criticizes Weber for positing *Verstehen* as a first step to causal analysis, defining "sociological law" as "a statistical regularity which corresponds to an intelligible intended meaning" (Winch, 1958: 113). In Winch's view, documenting the observable regularity of a form of human behavior will never bring us closer to its sociological meaning; it can at best verify the impressions qualifying certain observations. The final analytical problem for sociology is still the achievement of an "unreflective sensitivity" to the nonreflective practical understanding being studied and then explication of its logical structures purely on its own terms.

5. Garfinkel's "ethnomethodology" is perhaps the fullest realization of *Verstehen* sociology on both the Weberian and Schutzian levels of explication. The focus on the observable and reportable practices of actors is methodologically geared to the generation of sociological claims only in terms of what is available for these actors, irrespective of the occurrence of sociological analysis. This analytical constraint appears to satisfy Weber's call for "adequacy at the level of meaning." On the other hand, Schutz's effort to grasp the constitution of social structure in human practice is operationalized in an empirically rigorous fashion by the ethnomethodological program of analysis. Social structure is now grasped as it is "locally produced," and no presumptions are made about this structure outside of the pretheoretical framework of that production (Garfinkel, 1967; Heritage, 1984; Sharrock and Anderson, 1986).

6. By the turn of the twentieth century, the behaviorists' physiological notion of habit as an acquired neurological "reflex" or "response" predominated within psychological discourse. John Watson used the concept of habit to reduce all problems of human behavior and consciousness to problems of matter (or what B.F. Skinner has referred to as "dead matter in motion"). Thinking itself is reduced to objectively observable operations of the "tongue, throat, and laryngeal muscles...moving in habitual trains" (Watson,

quoted in Camic, 1986: 1068). Camic notes that during the early part of this century, before sociology had gained general acceptance in the United States as an autonomous discipline, American sociologists incorporated the psychologists' physiological conception of habit into their formulations of social life. Following World War I, however, both American and European sociologists abandoned references to habit in order to ward off the "extreme behaviorism [that] threatened to dominate the sociological scene" (Camic, 1986: 1075). The concept of habit is a "casualty" of sociology's struggle for autonomous academic status.

The cases of Durkheim and Weber hold special interest, since conceptions of habit that are broader than that of the behaviorists figure quite prominently in both of their writings. Yet both Durkheim and Weber eventually dropped their references to habit in order to differentiate the sociological focus on morality and reason from the psychological focus on automatic reflexes. Camic suggests that in this sense both Durkheim and Weber compromised their theoretical frameworks in the interests of interdisciplinary politics.

Camic's focus on the rise and decline of the concept of habit as a paradigmatic case of academic politics is quite interesting, as are his observations on the hitherto unacknowledged centrality of conceptions of habit in the writings of Durkheim and Weber. A problem with his discussion is that it tends to equate notions of habituality that are quite different from one another. For instance, the article makes passing reference to Bourdieu's concept of "habitus" (mentioning Bourdieu's coauthored study of education, rather than *Outline of a Theory of Practice*, where the concept of habitus receives its most direct elaboration), suggesting that Bourdieu "revives" Durkheim's and Weber's conceptions of habitus (Camic, 1986: 1046). The fact remains that both Durkheim's and Weber's uses of the concept are vague, referring to general aspects of "character" or "perspective." Neither Durkheim nor Weber employs the concept of habitus to develop theories of the habitual structure and dynamics of social life. Bourdieu devotes an entire text to the problem, and the results are a theoretical approach to social position and everyday practice that amounts to an understanding of habit that cannot be found in the works of either Durkheim or Weber.

Camic also pays little attention to the phenomenological approaches to habit mentioned in his article. Brief references to Schutz, Berger and Luckmann, Dewey, and Kestenbaum are made without acknowledgement of the distinction between "uses" of the concept of habit and studies of the dynamics of habit as a fundamental structure of experience. It is in the work of these and other writers that such studies are made; in a discussion of the importance of a concept of habit for sociological theory these studies might have been addressed with more than passing acknowledgment.

7. In his *Formal and Transcendental Logic* Husserl responds to the susceptibility of the phenomenological notion of transcendental subjectivity to the charge of solipsism as follows: "For children in philosophy, this may be a dark corner haunted by the spectres of solipsism and, perhaps, of psychologism, of relativism. The true philosopher, instead of running away, will prefer to fill the dark corner with light" (Husserl, 1969: 237). I try to meet this challenge by following Merleau-Ponty in his efforts to rescue the problem of intersubjectivity from that of intentional constitution.

8. This is not to suggest that Goffman's work is to be viewed *only* in terms of the Cooley-Mead tradition. In all of his writings Goffman can be seen to be borrowing from and refining elements of a variety of sociological perspectives, and he grew tired of critics who attempted to label his work according to single paradigms and then criticized him for deviating from these paradigms. See, for instance, Goffman's reply to a review of his *Frame Analysis* (Goffman, 1981b).

Chapter 2

1. For a discussion of Schutz's reformulation of the study of knowledge in sociology, see John Heeren, "Alfred Schutz and the Sociology of Common-Sense Knowledge" (1970).

The "constructionist" perspective of social reality developed by Berger and Luckmann in *The Social Construction of Reality*, as well as the ethnomethodological program for analyses of everyday life, are perhaps the principal areas of phenomenological sociology, and both are rooted directly within Schutz's focus on practically functional knowledge (Berger and Luckmann, 1966; Garfinkel, 1967). Sharrock and Anderson write: "It was in the 1960's that Schutz began to receive attention, and the rapid rediscovery of his writings was probably due more to...*The Social Construction of Reality* than to the notoriety of ethnomethodology." Although Garfinkel may not be "more of a true or approved inheritor of Schutz's tradition," Sharrock and Anderson believe Garfinkel "saw the potential for a much more radical rethinking of sociological ideas in the work of Schutz" (Sharrock and Anderson, 1986: 11). See Psathas (1980) for a similar point of view and a more detailed comparison of the writings of Schutz and Garfinkel.

2. See, for instance, Kohák, 1978; Madison, 1981; James Schmidt, 1985; and James Edie's introduction to *The Primacy of Perception* (Merleau-Ponty, 1964a).

3. For a systematic treatment of differences between the "early" and "later" perspectives of Husserl, see the chapter, "Phenomenology and the Sciences of Man," in Merleau-Ponty, 1964a.

4. The sense in which I use the term "contact" is similar to Paul Goodman's in his rewrite of the introduction to F. Perls' *Gestalt Therapy* (1951). Goodman writes: "Let us call the 'self' the system of contacts at any moment" (235).

Also see James Sheridan's discussion of experiential contact in *Once More—From the Middle* (1973).

5. I agree with Samuel Mallin, who views Merleau-Ponty's *The Visible and the Invisible* as a series of ontological elaborations of insights developed in the *Phenomenology of Perception*. For an opposing view, see Madison, 1981 and Schmidt, 1985. Madison and Schmidt both claim that Merleau-Ponty's later works represent a break from his earlier interests in the philosophy of consciousness.

6. *La Structure du Comportement* was published originally in 1942. The original edition of *Phénoménologie de la Perception* appeared in 1945.

7. Merleau-Ponty writes: "The intentional relation shows us

the intentional threads that bind the phenomenal body to its surroundings and finally will reveal to us the perceiving subject as the perceived world" (Merleau-Ponty, 1962: 72). Merleau-Ponty essentially locates the pure subjectivity of experience at the level of what, in *Experience and Judgment*, Husserl calls the "passive pregivenness" of the life-world (Husserl, 1973: 29-30).

8. John Dewey also focuses a theory of habit on the distinction between "having" and "knowing." Dewey writes: "*being* and *having* things in ways other than knowing them, in ways never identified with knowing them, exist, and are preconditions of reflection and knowledge. *Being* angry, stupid, wise, inquiring; *having* sugar, the light of day, money, houses and lands, friends, laws, masters, subjects, pain and job, occur in dimensions incommensurable to knowing these things which we are and have and use, and which have and use us. Their existence is unique, and, strictly speaking, indescribable; they can *only be* and be *had*, and then be pointed to in reflection" (Dewey, 1925: 18-19).

John Findlay's distinction between "fulfilled" and "validated" meaning corresponds to this distinction between having and knowing (Findlay, 1963).

9. For an elaboration of the phenomenological meaning of habit as developed in the writings of Merleau-Ponty and Dewey, see Victor Kestenbaum, 1977. Kestenbaum's text introduced me to, and is central to my understanding of, the phenomenon of habit.

10. In Dewey's early essay "Interpretations of the Savage Mind" he writes: "Hunter and hunted are the factors of a single tension; the mental situations cannot be defined except in terms of both" (Dewey, 1931: 184). This essay attacks types of analysis conducted by Herbert Spencer, for instance, where the practices of primitive cultures are viewed comparatively with modern practices and interpreted solely with respect to their relative deficiencies. Dewey's analysis of the hunter's experience in terms of the means-ends drama of his cultural perspective—the intertwining of all political, intellectual, and aesthetic aspects of life with the pure, subsistence circumstance of the hunter—establishes an early basis for his theory of habit. Dewey concludes the essay with a remarkable passage, suggesting that a historical analysis of the

social division of labor be grounded in a "genetic psychology" of habit: "to show the purely immediate personal adjustment of habit to direct satisfaction, in the savage, became transformed through the introduction of impersonal generalized objective instrumentalities and ends; how it ceased to be immediate and became loaded and surcharged with a content which forced personal want, initiative, effort, and satisfaction further and further apart, putting all kinds of social divisions of labor, intermediate agencies, and objective contents between them. This is the problem of the formation of mental patterns appropriate to agricultural, military, professional, and technological and trade pursuits, and the reconstruction and overlaying of the original hunting scheme" (Dewey, 1931: 187).

Kestenbaum provides an extensive discussion of the importance of this essay in the development of Dewey's theory of habit, giving special attention to the concept of a "single tension" between self and world (1977).

11. It is worth noting that Husserl's notion of habituality in his later writings is quite similar to Dewey's and Merleau-Ponty's, although he never fully incorporates it into his theory of experience. In *Experience and Judgment*, Husserl writes: "...commonplace sense is in no way related purely and simply to cognitive behavior; taken in its greatest generality, it is related, rather, to a habituality *(Habitualität)* which lends to him who is provided with it, to him who is 'experienced,' assurance in decision and action in the situations of life...." The translators of *Experience and Judgment* note that "habituality in this text does not have its occasional and informal English meaning, but should be understood as designating, rather, the philosophical concept (*'Habitualität,'* also translated as *'habitus'*) of an acquired intelligent disposition" (Husserl, 1973: 52).

12. While Sartre follows Søren Kierkegaard's rejection of the classical philosophical idea of absolute "truths" or "essences" hidden beneath human existence, he also opposes Kierkegaard's belief that within human subjectivity lie the "inner" *potentiae* of existence that are never fully "externalized" in action.

13. See Dewey's discussion of the rigidification of habit in

Democracy and Education (Dewey, 1916); also, see Paul Ricoeur's discussion of what he calls the "fall into automatism" in *Freedom and Nature: The Voluntary and the Involuntary* (Ricoeur, 1966). Ricoeur's discussion of habit is consistent with Dewey's and Merleau-Ponty's, if not as central to his philosophical perspective. Ricoeur writes: "To reflect on habit always means to refer to the time of life, to the holds which a living being offers to time, and the holds which, thanks to time, he acquires on his body and 'through' it on things" (Ricoeur, 1966: 280-281).

14. Merleau-Ponty writes: "In every focusing moment my body unites present, past, and future, it secretes time....My body takes possession of time; it brings into existence a past and a future for a present, it is not a thing, but creates time instead of submitting to it" (Merleau-Ponty, 1962: 239-240).

15. "Habits are our inherence in a field of time; through their functioning there is a concretion of past, present, and future" (Kestenbaum, 1977: 91).

16. In a comparative study of the philosophies of Schutz and Dewey, Webb argues that Schutz's concept of "because-motives" is similar to Dewey's notion of habit. In Schutz's view all social action is comprehensible in terms of either "because-motives" or "in-order-to-motives." The latter are a subject's ongoing sense of the meaning of his action with respect to its implications and usefulness for what will follow. "Because-motives" are, on the other hand, the "lived experience temporally prior to the project" (Webb, 1976: 80). As Webb sees it, "because-motives" are the prereflective "awakenings" of interests that are funded by habits; this is why Schutz refers to them as "imposed": Motivation at this level "is not a particularly voluntary act," but one in which objects of the world "awaken expectancies of habit" (Webb, 1976: 81).

Webb demonstrates a parallel between Schutz's theory of motivation and Dewey's theory of the intensification of habit in present experience. However, Webb might have added that since the phenomenon of habit is, according to Schutz, strictly a "possession of my stock of knowledge" (Webb, 1976: 80), Schutz is never able to grasp it as an intrinsic dynamic of prereflective experience. Schutz merely infers the existence of a latent store of knowledge lying behind experience, whereas Merleau-Ponty and Dewey describe the workings of habits as the very texture of the dialectic between person and world in immediate experience.

Chapter 3

1. Thomas Luckmann offers an interesting discussion of Husserl's theory of intersubjectivity in an essay entitled "On the Boundaries of the Social World" (1983a). Luckmann brings an ethnological sensitivity to bear on Husserl's theory of intersubjectivity and argues that Husserl has no grounds for assuming that the transcendental ego has a sense of its own humanness. It follows that Husserl's basing of a theory of intersubjectivity on a subject's projection (or "appresentation") of its own human characteristics to another is also unfounded. Luckmann goes on to claim that there is in fact a universal appresentation of subjectivity outside of oneself that is phenomenologically prior to the appresentation of a specifically human alter ego: "All things encountered in the life-world are experienced in a synthesis of their perceived qualities with the appresented sense 'living body.' This sense refers to something that has a *durée*, not merely a location; an inside is appresented to the perceptible outside." Hence, "the sense 'human being' is a modification of the primary sense 'living body'" (Luckmann, 1983a: 46). The ways that this primary sense becomes restricted to particular environmental phenomena and excluded from others are a consequence of historicoculturally specific forms of socialization, which is why there is enormous cultural variation with respect to what in the world is considered animated—i.e., endowed with subjectivity. There are obviously things in the environment that are less mobile than others; these are not "synchronous" with the rhythms of one's consciousness and, hence, lose "plausibility" as objects of the original "universal projection." The appresented subjectivity of these objects endures only if "socially observed institutionally supported interpretations explain away [their] physiognomic immobility" (Luckmann, 1983a: 56). Hence, when Luckmann criticizes Husserl's restriction of the meaning of intersubjectivity, the implication is that Husserl was unable to shed from his phenomenological reflections the presuppositions of his par-

ticular cultural heritage. Luckmann means to free phenomenology from this restriction in order to clear the way for an inquiry into various historicocultural restrictions of the universal projection.

Luckmann's thesis of the "universal projection" is interesting; yet there is no phenomenological reflection on the structure of human consciousness to support the thesis. He accepts as a matter of course the Husserlian idea of the apperceptive transfer of sense by which an ego posits an alter ego. After citing ethnological evidence of various cultures that perceive nonhuman phenomena to be endowed with consciousness, he deduces that the apperceptive transfer of sense within the transcendental sphere is indiscriminate in the sense of being applicable to anything in the life-world. The phenomenological grounds for this deduction are not clear. It seems to me that Luckmann's ethnological argument provides a sound basis for calling into question Husserl's central claim that the existence of other subjects in the life-world is based upon an apperceptive "pairing" of another's body with one's own. However, Luckmann opts instead to modify Husserl's theory of inter-subjectivity with the notion of the "universal projection."

For an interesting comparison of Husserl's and William James' theories of intersubjectivity, see Richard Stevens (1974). Stevens argues that a subject's realization of the convertibility of his perspectival position in the spatial world with another subject is, for both Husserl and James, at the heart of intersubjective identification.

2. This line of argument was influenced by Ortega y Gasset's criticism of Husserl's theory of intersubjectivity (Schutz, 1962c: 143).

Schutz conducts his most extensive analysis and criticism of Husserl's theory of intersubjectivity in "The Problem of Transcendental Intersubjectivity in Husserl" (1966b).

3. For Schutz, intersubjectivity is the basic construct of common sense by which one takes for granted the existence of fellow human beings who share a common world of sense and significance. With respect to one's relationship to others, this involves two typifications that together comprise what Schutz calls the "general thesis of the reciprocity of perspectives": 1) I take for granted that

my spatial and temporal position in the world, my "here," offers to my senses the same objective world, with an intelligibility that remains obvious, that exists over "there"—from the other's point of view. In other words, I assume that our standpoints are interchangeable and that others assume the same; 2) I also take for granted that other persons are, like myself, practical beings and are able to make choices on the basis of what is useful for our respective purposes. I recognize the personal ("biographical") differences between us, but assume that for the practical purposes which conjoin us we share common "systems of relevancies." I take for granted that not merely I, but *we*, share "ways of life" and ways of achieving typical ends in typical situations (Schutz and Luckmann, 1974: 60; Schutz, 1962a: 11-12).

4. Schutz makes this same point in a critique of Husserl's *Ideen II* (Schutz, 1966a). Husserl suggests that communication is the basis of sociality. Schutz contends that "communication presupposes already a social interrelationship on which it is founded, such as the relationship of being 'tuned in' one upon the other..." (Schutz, 1966a: 38). Any vehicles of communication, whether verbal or nonverbal, owe the possibility of their intelligibility to a "common environment" and, therefore, cannot constitute it.

For an extensive discussion of Schutz's various uses of the concept of the "We-relation" see Parsons, 1973.

5. Schutz is expanding upon Weber's distinction between "subjective" and "objective" meaning. " 'Subjective meaning' refers to whatever 'goes on,' intellectually and emotionally, in an individual who produces something—anything: A sentence, a cry, a building, a string quartet; it refers to what the individual means by the producing. 'Subjective meaning' contrasts with 'objective meaning,' which is what the individual's producing means to me who wants to understand it, irrespective of what it means to the producer, irrespective of its subjective meaning" (Wolff, 1984: 200).

6. "I apprehend the lived experiences of another only through signitive-symbolic representation, regarding either his body or some cultural artifact he has produced as a 'field of expression' for these experiences...the bodily movements are perceived not only as physical events but also as a sign that the other person is having

certain lived experiences which he is expressing through these movements. My intentional gaze is directed right through my perceptions of his bodily movements to his lived experiences lying behind them and signified by them" (Schutz, 1932: 100-101).

7. Merleau-Ponty is attacking Husserl's reference to Saint Augustine at the conclusion of Husserl's fifth "Cartesian Meditation" (1960). See Madison, 1981:215. Kohák argues that when Saint Augustine speaks of a return to the "inner man," he is not referring to a "subjective" turn away from the world: "The crucial distinction is not between an 'outer' and an 'inner' reality but, as Bergson recognized, between understanding any and all reality *from within* and explaining it superficially from without" (Kohák, 1984: 207). Kohák argues that the failure of Husserl's readers to understand his appeal to Saint Augustine in this sense is indicative of their general misunderstanding of Husserl's notion of transcendental subjectivity.

8. Goffman notes that the face is especially vulnerable to lack of control in this regard: "Facial expression is capable of extremely rapid changes and extremely delicate shadings. It can be exquisitely responsive to the passing moment and is required to be (indeed, one could speak of a facial frame, for the face will ordinarily be ordered in keeping with the framed activity in progress). It is through this expression—more constantly than any other—that the individual is obliged to demonstrate appropriate involvement in and regard for the scene at hand. Yet necessarily this field of expression is a labile, unstable thing. It can be deformed by any perceivable wind. It is this screen of responsiveness that must be examined functionally" (Goffman, 1974: 349).

Simmel celebrates the communicative power and aesthetic unity of the face. He writes, "a change which is limited, actually or apparently, to one element of the face—a curl of the lips, an upturning of the nose, a way of looking, a frown—immediately modifies its entire character and expression. Aesthetically, there is no other part of the body whose wholeness can as easily be destroyed by the disfigurement of only one of its elements.... Within the perceptible world, there is no other structure like the human face which merges such a great variety of shapes and surfaces into an absolute unity of meaning" (Simmel, 1959: 276-277).

9. The lack of sensitivity to the situational structure of inter-subjectivity is pointed out by Kurt H. Wolff's observation that, when Schutz distinguishes between those with whom I share physical presence ("consociates") and those who live at the same time as me but do not share physical presence ("contemporaries"), he fails to conduct any phenomenological inquiry into the experiential "difference between somebody being with me and not being with me" (Wolff, 1982: 9).

10. John Dewey states the same idea in different terms: "The epidermis is only in the most superficial way an indication of where an organism ends and its environment begins. There are things inside of the body that are foreign to it, and there are things outside of it that belong to it de jure, if not de facto" (Dewey, 1958: 58).

11. Merleau-Ponty is in fundamental disagreement with Sartre, who rejects the idea of intersubjectivity altogether by arguing that the social encounter is best characterized as a context for a mutual denial of subjectivity. Sartre's view is based on the idea that when others perceive us we experience self-objectification, becoming suddenly conscious of ourselves as "things" located within a spatiotemporal world. The social encounter is therefore essentially a confrontation between self and other, because one's pure subjectivity—the perpetual freedom to engage possibilities beyond existing circumstances—is always stripped by the other, whose perception fixes the self as a finite and fully constituted entity among other entities in the world. Merleau-Ponty agrees that when we are aware of ourselves seen and heard by others, we may experience the objectification Sartre refers to, but "only if [we] withdraw into the core of our thinking nature, if we...make [one another] into an inhuman gaze, if [we feel our] actions to be not taken up and understood, but observed as if they were an insect's" (Merleau-Ponty, 1962: 361). That is to say, self-objectification is the consequence of an act of reflection rather than an essential property of the encounter prior to reflection. By taking the denial of subjectivity through objectification to be intrinsic to the structure of the social encounter, Sartre shares with Schutz a failure to grasp the intersubjectivity of situations that precedes and is the foundation of

our ability to posit our own and another's body as objects of thought.

For a critique of Sartre's position on the phenomenon of intersubjectivity that is consistent with Merleau-Ponty's, see Grene, 1959. Sartre only discusses intersubjectivity negatively, in terms of a conflict between selves, or, as Grene puts it, in terms of "a circle of conflicts" between "myself as subject and the other who sees me as object, between my freedom and its destruction in another's possession of me" (Grene, 1959: 80). Grene argues that the unity of selves seems just as much a possibility of the social encounter as is conflict; in fact, it is the ground for the possibility of conflict. For instance, Grene does not reject Sartre's claim that conflict is a basic relation between parent and child, but she suggests that the original togetherness of the family is the foundation for the development of such conflict.

Grene extends this argument to Sartre's discussion of the problems of choice (value generation) with respect to the self's relations to others. Sartre's error is that he ultimately reduces choice to a private phenomenon, ignoring the intersubjectivity of the situation in which choices are made. Sartre gives the example of a boy who must "create his own values in his situation" in choosing between running off to England to join the "Free French," or staying home with his mother. Grene agrees, but objects to Sartre's omission of the nexus of past and present decisions and acts of both mother and son that comprise the situation in which the creation of values is possible. Grene is arguing that Sartre and existentialists in general miss a deeper sense of subjectivity, the sense that, situationally, subjectivity is intersubjectivity. So it is perhaps true that the boy's choices are not, when understood in a purely existential sense, predetermined by prior values. Yet this does not mean that the act of choosing is private, or isolated from others' acts and choices.

Finally, Grene notes that with no real existential grounding of intersubjectivity, Sartre ignores or discounts a central medium for the genuine fulfillment of human possibilities: the formation of meaningful social ties. The quest for interpersonal intimacy is not "only—though it is in part—a surrender to convention, a desire to be what society and instinct combine in urging against the deeper claims of freedom. It is, beyond that, the sense of wanting the completion of one's self in others which is just as genuine in human consciousness as is the ultimate privacy which existentialism prefers to stress" (Grene, 1959: 88).

Schutz also discusses and criticizes Sartre's theory of intersubjectivity in "Sartre's Theory of the Alter Ego" (1962d). Schutz argues that Sartre's position on intersubjectivity fails to provide grounds for comprehending "the concrete understanding of the Other whose existence is taken for granted" (Schutz, 1962d: 199).

12. For a critique of Scheler's position, see Merleau-Ponty, 1973a. Also see Owens, 1970 for a comprehensive discussion of Scheler's, Sartre's, and Dietrich von Hilderbrand's theories of intersubjectivity.

13. Paul Goodman observes that the view that speech "represents" prior thoughts as opposed to being a mode of thinking, "one way of taking and making a present situation," is not only a philosophical, but also a pedagogical error: "In my observation, too much going to school and being quizzed inhibits people from speaking naturally; instead of saying what they have to say, they have to figure out beforehand what the teacher wants them to say" (Goodman, 1971: 13).

14. For elaborations of Merleau-Ponty's notion of expression as a mode of awareness in an intersubjective context see Gillan, 1973. Gillan writes: "The signifying intention which gives rise to expression and which one usually associates with the movements of conscious thought is not a movement on a level other than words, but a 'gap'—an absence of sense felt in what has already been said and what demands to be spoken—whose only adequate response to what it wants to say consists in speaking" (Gillan, 1973: 50). Also see Ihde, 1973 for a discussion of Merleau-Ponty's concept of the "pregnant silence" which is the background of all speech.

15. For a Wittgensteinian argument against the idea of expression as a "cognitive representation" of emotion, see Coulter, 1989.

16. Husserl claims "fiction is the source whence the knowledge of 'eternal truths' draws its sustenance" (Husserl, 1931: 184). By "eternal truths," Husserl means nothing else than pregiven struc-

tures and principles of human experience—or the essential foundations of an inhabited world being and becoming meaningful.

17. André Malraux writes: Style is "a call for and not a consequence of a way of seeing" (Merleau-Ponty, 1964b: 53).

Chapter 4

1. Cooley's and Mead's theories of self can be viewed as elaborations of William James' concept of the "social self." James' argument that the person possesses "as many social selves as there are individuals who recognize him" (James, 1890: 294) certainly anticipates and informs Mead's development of "role theory." However, it is important to note that for James the "social self" is only one of three dimensions of selfhood; there is also the "material self," comprised of the objects within the material environment that individuals possess as integral to their existence and identity, and the "spiritual self," which includes the various, typical aspects of a person's mannerisms, perspective, and capabilities. Only the concept of the "social self" retains central importance for Cooley and Mead.

2. Cooley beings his famous essay "The Meaning of 'I' " by locating the "empirical self"—"the self that can be apprehended or verified by ordinary observation" (Cooley, 1922: 168)—as the central concern of a sociology of self. This is the meaning of self that is represented in speech by the first person singular pronouns "I," "me," "mine," "myself," and it is precisely the social character of their intelligibility and use to which Cooley directs his attention. Cooley acknowledges the existence of other conceptions of self in philosophical thought, but implies that these are little more than analytical derivations of the fundamental meanings that are manifested by personal pronouns. Thus, the philosophical notion of the "pure ego" is dismissed as a metaphorical obscuration of what "should not be very much more difficult to get hold of than other facts of mind" (Cooley, 1922: 169).

3. Denzin calls the embedding of self-reflexive awareness "self-lodging," the process through which "humans translate crucial

features of their own identity into selves, memories, and imaginations of other relevant others. It is in this way that Cooley's proposition that the other exists in our imagination of him comes to life. By lodging the self in interaction and in the selves of others, a reciprocal bond is created and the firm foundations for future relations are established" (Denzin, 1970: 262).

4. Six years after the publication of *Human Nature and the Social Order* (first published in 1902), Cooley published an empirical study of his third child's development of the use of "self-words." The study refines many of his earlier statements about children's uses of first-person pronouns and retains the same argument about the relationship between "self-feeling" and "self-consciousness" (Cooley, 1908). As Cooley reports it, his child's development of the use of first-person pronouns at different ages is uneven, occurring in flashes rather than in a smoothly progressive fashion. This leads Cooley to disparage early uses of these pronouns as merely "imitative," with no "real sense of the meaning of 'I' " (Cooley, 1908: 347). Paule Verdet makes the interesting argument that Cooley has fallen for the trappings of a rigid model of psychological development, failing to recognize the following implications of his research: "Clearly, the child's progress is far from continuous. She seems to proceed by sudden insights which are not immediately maintained. This suggests that the process at work is not maturation but literally creation, through selection from the infinitely varied and complex messages coming from her social environment" (Paule Verdet, unpublished notes). I am grateful to Professor Verdet for directing me to Cooley's study and for providing me with her interesting remarks.

5. It might be objected that Mead recognizes this issue when he distinguishes between the phenomena of "I" and "me" in experience. It is true that Mead conceives of the "I" as the undetermined and always potentially novel response of the individual to immediate circumstances. The "I" can be contrasted with the "me," defined as the already established "organized set of attitudes of others which one himself assumes" (Mead, 1934: 175). Yet Mead repeats throughout his discussion of the self that what he is calling the "I" is to be understood in terms of the experience of self-

consciousness—of taking the attitudes of others. The "I" is in this sense one's response to the world as it exists for "me." Mead argues that one may "adjust himself unconsciously to those about him," but he adds that this is the level of the "bare organic response" of the "organism." As far as I can tell, Mead never directly addresses the problem of the prereflective occasion and context for self-consciousness.

6. This intrusion is an example of what Goffman calls a "territorial violation," which applies to any event in which someone disrupts or intrudes upon something that others implicitly claim as part of their rightful occupation of the environment (Goffman, 1971).

7. The counterpart to expression given-off is "expression given," which includes any words or gestures used to openly convey information. Expressions given differ from expressions given-off in that they are meant to be perceived as intentionally communicative (Goffman, 1959: 2).

8. Another contrast between Simmel and Goffman would be on the topic of "tact." Simmel suggests that "where no external or immediate egoistic interests direct self-regulation of the individual in his personal relations with others, it is tact that fulfills this regulatory function" (Simmel, 1950: 45). Goffman argues that "tact" is a "protective practice" in the sense that it is the form of "expression given-off" designed to protect others from embarrassment. For instance, a woman at a college mixer might pretend to be involved in the business of those seated next to her upon seeing the approach of a man she does not want to dance with. She thereby acts "tactfully," protecting him from the embarrassment of completing his approach and being rejected (Schwartz and Lever, 1976). Yet Goffman is careful to note that tact is performed largely in the interests of *defending oneself* against the negative impressions of others, where one might be seen as nasty or rude. Thus, tact does, as Simmel says, fulfill a "regulatory function," but that function is, following Goffman, to be understood largely in terms of the self-reflexive monitoring of conduct.

In any case, Simmel's notion of "playing" society through

sociability certainly clears the way for Goffman's formulations. In fact, Simmel leaves open the question of what particular interests will motivate this play when he writes: "the deep spring which feeds this realm and its play does not lie in these forms [self-perpetuating principles of social relations], but exclusively in the vitality of concrete individuals, with all their feelings and attractions, convictions and impulses" (Simmel, 1950: 55).

9. See for instance the final two paragraphs of *The Presentation of Self in Everyday Life*, where Goffman suggests that the metaphorical framework of dramaturgical analysis is similar to "scaffolds" that "are to build other things with, and should be erected with an eye to taking them down" (Goffman, 1959: 254).

10. The notion of ritualization may be viewed as Goffman's way of answering those who criticize him for positing the human being as a perpetually paranoid and conniving creature. Goffman wants to suggest that gestures serve discernible functions in the maintenance of social order, irrespective of the particular fears or motivations of individuals. It is debatable whether this adequately refutes Psathas' claim that, even in the absence of explicit statements about human intention, Goffman still presupposes certain attributes of individual, human nature (Psathas, 1977).

I agree with Bruce Wilshire, who argues that it is Goffman's superficial conception of *appearance* that leads him to presuppose an essentially nonsocial selfhood. Wilshire writes: "[Goffman's] notion of appearances harbors nominalism that assumes general senses are mere general names—mental shortcuts for blurring real differences among real things, which are always particular. Since an appearance is one particular thing, that of which it is the appearance must be another, and it is eminently that which can be concealed by the appearance.... Goffman asserts that what we glimpse is the 'look of one who is privately engaged in a difficult, treacherous task.' The task is that of 'impression management,' the manipulation of other 'presented' selves through the impressions of oneself which one gives them. So the naked face we glimpse must be a nonsocial or asocial one" (Wilshire, 1982: 274-275).

11. Giddens goes on to suggest that Goffman "shows us many of the things we 'know' about social convention, and other aspects

of society, but which we 'know' in a tacit rather than explicit sense" (Giddens, 1981: 169). For similar views on the power of Goffman's descriptive style see Berman, 1972; Bourdieu, 1984; Manning, 1980; Ricks, 1981.

12. It would be difficult, of course, to *prove* that the behavior described here contains what Goffman implies: an individual's orientation to having interrupted others. Indeed, it is entirely conceivable that a person might simply exit the setting without caring, much less acknowledging visibly, that he had ever entered it. Yet the issues of proof or "alternative readings" are beside the point; what matters is that Goffman's description is a plausible reading of experience under particular social circumstances. The theoretical problem is to ascertain precisely what he reveals about experience with this reading (cf. Chapter 6).

13. In *Garfinkel and Ethnomethodology* (1984) John Heritage argues that there is a "bias" within social encounters that is "favorable to the maintenance of bonds of solidarity between actors and which promotes the avoidance of conflict" (Heritage, 1984: 265). Heritage ultimately attributes this bias to a "concern for face" (Heritage, 1984: 268), in the sense in which that concern is formulated by Goffman. It is likely that many ethnomethodologists would oppose Heritage's appeal to Goffman, since in positing the existence of such a motivational force he has severed the direct analytical tie to "members' practices" that is at the cornerstone of the ethnomethodological paradigm. Yet his need to do so may point to the inability of any strictly interactionist perspective to account for the bias to maintain solidarity and stability within social circumstances. I believe that such a bias can be adequately comprehended only by seeing that, as argued in the previous chapter, subjectivity is essentially intersubjective by virtue of its fundamentally corporeal structure. The bias toward an orderliness in interaction is grounded in the singularly preobjective context that situates the expressive character of consciousness. It is not sufficient to say that individuals are biased toward protecting themselves as separate "faces," because what they are as "selves" is already instituted by the experiential circumstance of social copresence. Hence, the bias toward solidarity within interaction is, funda-

mentally, a disposition to inhabit the world, which we are historically and inescapably sensitive to inhabiting. Interactional orderliness, as it has been discovered and explored most comprehensively by Garfinkel and his followers, is rooted within the intersubjective structure of experience.

14. In another example of "remedial work" Goffman notes that on a subway a person "accidentally stepping on the toe of a seated passenger can maintain his rate of movement, turn his head back and hold out his arm and hand while he verbally excuses himself. The held-out hand, in effect, holds the offender in the remedial encounter even while his body is rapidly leaving it" (1971: 17). Does the person consider the possibilities of the other's negative judgments of him prior to or during his gesturing? Such possibilities are foreseeable and, no doubt, could be attended to and manipulated. Yet their very existence is contingent upon the situations in which they might arise as matters of awareness.

Indeed, the actions of the passenger on foot cannot be understood phenomenologically by referring solely to their overt orientation, or to what the ethnomethodological analyst of conversation would call their "recipient design." We must interpret the passenger's conduct in terms of the preobjective thickness of this world within which he is steeped. The moving passenger is disposed to gesture apologetically to the one who is seated, but only in the context of a larger, social copresence—a subtle yet pervasive form of intersubjective contact that saturates the unacquainted within a shared situation. Stepping on another's toes entails a surge of intersubjective intensity that occurs within this situation. The moving passenger holds the inadvertently heightened intensity of his and another's copresence with a gesture, and yet by pulling rapidly away he does so in the context of the more diffuse contact that situates the self that he is, as an embodiment of sensitivity within this social world.

15. This account of self-reflexivity makes it possible to ground Mead's theory of the "generalized other" phenomenologically. Mead demonstrates that a sense of self need not be bound to perceptions of specific individuals, nor to any specific face-to-face encounter. In our example, the intruder's expressions embody

sensitivity to his presence within a "group," not necessarily to any particular members of the group. It follows that any thoughts of his own rudeness need not be restricted to his perceptions of specific individuals and may even extend beyond those present to a more "general" group within which he might earn a particular reputation. Mead would say that the intruder has acquired an understanding of the rights and obligations of "society" and therefore can "take the attitudes of others" in a "generalized" way. The ephemeral metaphor of "taking the attitude of others" can give way to a more concrete understanding of what Mead alludes to by recognizing that a sensitivity to inhabiting the presence of others is foundational to a consciousness of their expressive behavior and thoughts. This means that an orientation to the expectations of a group—as well as to self-awareness in the context of the group—is grounded in the preobjective structure of intersubjective experience.

Chapter 5

1. Anthony Giddens argues that "macro" approaches, such as Durkheimian and Parsonian functionalism or the structualism of Ferdinand de Saussure and Claude Lévi-Strauss, share a prioritization of "objective" structure or systems over "subjective" actions in their theories of social existence. The "micro" approaches of, for instance, symbolic interactionism or ethnomethodology tend to ignore broader issues of the reproduction of sociohistorical systems in favor of their more immediate focus on social interaction (Giddens, 1979).

2. The title of Bourdieu's rewrite of *Outline of a Theory of Practice* is *Le Sens Pratique* (1979).

3. See Ostrow, 1981 for an earlier development of this claim in the context of a phenomenological theory of culture.

4. Marcel Mauss introduced a similar usage of the term "habitus" in his work on culturally specific patterns of "body technique." Like Bourdieu, he was careful to note that the term refers to more than routine physical behaviors: "I use the Latin word...*habitus*. The word translates infinitely better than *'habitude'*

(habit or custom), the *'exis,'* the 'acquired ability' and 'faculty' of Aristotle (who was a psychologist). It does not designate those metaphysical *habitudes*, that mysterious 'memory,' the subjects of volumes of short and famous theses. These 'habits' do not vary just with individuals and their imitations; they vary especially between societies, educations, proprieties, fashions, prestiges. In them we should see the techniques and work of collective and individual practical reason rather than, in the ordinary way, merely the soul and its repetitive faculties" (Mauss, 1979: 101).

Bourdieu's concept of habitus is also reminiscent of, although I believe it significantly deepens, Mannheim's theory of "perspective." By the term "perspective," Mannheim denotes the "one-sidedness" of knowledge, which is always produced within and sustained by a particular socio-historical setting. Although it is true that Mannheim's sociology of knowledge is generally confined to ideas that are thematic and thematically related to one another, the notion of perspective is clearly more encompassing in its implications for a theory of human consciousness. What seems particularly compelling about this notion, while being realized more fully in Bourdieu's discussions of habitus, is its implications for a sociological grounding of consciousness that extends beyond a sociology of knowledge. Mannheim himself suggests that the concept of perspective "signifies the manner in which one views an object, what one perceives in it, and how one construes it in his thinking. Perspective, therefore, is something more than a merely formal determination of thinking. It refers also to qualitative elements in the structure of thought, elements which must necessarily be overlooked by a purely formal logic. It is precisely these factors which are responsible for the fact that two persons, even if they apply the same formal-logical rules, e.g., the law of contradiction or the formula of the syllogism, in an identical manner, may judge the same object very differently" (Mannheim, 1936: 272).

5. In offering class condition as an example of one's social position Bourdieu concurs with Weber's and Mannheim's arguments that socioeconomic class represents one among several possible clusters of social relations. The problem is "one of determining which of these affiliations are decisive in fixing

perspectives, models of thought, definitions of the group, etc." (Merton, 1957: 470).

Mannheim does not disagree with Marx's claim that all "social groups arise from and are transformed as parts of the more basic conditions of production and domination" (Mannheim, 1936: 276). For Mannheim, this does not obviate the sociological significance of enduring social relations in their existing noneconomic forms. Bourdieu agrees with Weber's and Mannheim's similar concession to Marx that "of all social groups and units class stratification is the most significant" (Mannheim, 1936: 276); yet along with Weber and Mannheim, Bourdieu rejects any form of economic determinism that reduces noneconomic social groupings to mere derivations of class distinctions.

It is worth noting that Marx also recognizes, but never succeeds in adequately accounting for the fact, that the ideas expressed within a given social class are not necessarily derived exclusively from persons originally belonging to it. Marx observes that during the transition from feudalism to capitalism a section of the nobility "went over to the bourgeoisie," just as in Marx's own time a "portion of the bourgeoisie goes over to the proletariat, and in particular, a portion of the bourgeoisie ideologists, who have raised themselves to the level of comprehending theoretically the historical movement as a whole" (Marx, 1955: 20).

6. Merleau-Ponty makes a similar argument when, explicating what he views as the phenomenological sense of Marx's philosophical materialism, he writes: "The economy of a time gives rise to an ideology because it is lived by men who seek their realization in it. In one sense, this economy limits their views; but in another it is their surface contact with being, their experience, and it can happen, as it happened to Marx himself, that they do not merely submit to this economy but understand it and thus virtually go beyond it" (Merleau-Ponty, 1964c: 132).

7. Bourdieu borrows this term from Goffman's *Asylums* (1961b).

8. A preliminary analysis of the following example can be found in Ostrow, 1987.

9. Bourdieu uses the concept of "tempo" in order to charac-

terize practically situated time, "which is made up of incommensurable islands of duration, each with its own rhythm, the time that flies or drags, depending on what one is *doing*" (Bourdieu, 1977: 105).

10. Examples of such studies are Apple, 1979; Bernstein, 1977; Carnoy, 1975; Gintis & Bowles, 1976; Karabel and Halsey, 1977; Spring, 1972; Spring, 1976.

11. "I am not conscious of being working class or middle class simply because, as a matter of fact, I sell my labor or, equally as a matter of fact, because my interests are bound up with capitalism, nor do I become one or the other on the day on which I elect to view history in the light of the class struggle: What happens is that 'I exist as working class' or 'I exist as middle class' in the first place, and it is this mode of dealing with the world and society which provides both the motives for my revolutionary or conservative projects and my explicit judgements of the type: 'I am working class' or 'I am middle class,' without its being possible to deduce the former from the latter, or *vice versa*. What makes me a proletarian is not the economic system or society considered as systems of impersonal forces, but these institutions as I carry them within me and experience them; nor is it an intellectual operation devoid of motive, but my way of being in the world within this institutional framework" (Merleau-Ponty, 1962: 443).

In his superb study of Merleau-Ponty's social phenomenology John O'Neill writes: "Embodied consciousness never experiences an original innocence to which any violence would be an irreparable harm; it knows only different kinds of violence. For consciousness finds itself already engaged in the world, in definite situations in which its resources are never merely its own but derive from the exploitation of its position as the husband of this woman, the child of these parents, the master of these slaves" (1970: 81-82).

Chapter 6

1. The prejudice of determinate being is as prevalent within contemporary interpretive sociology as within so-called "positivist" sociology. Here the case of ethnomethodology proves instructive.

Ethnomethodology opposes any formulations that posit social phenomena apart from what is manifestly present within the nontheoretical context of persons' everyday practices. Only those phenomena that are *observable and reportable* by and for non-theorizing "members" of the social world—irrespective of the occurrence of sociological analysis—count as valid sociological "data." Yet ethnomethodology also shares with the various paradigms that it opposes an insistence on the spuriousness of any claims about human reality that do not presuppose its reducibility to determinate objects—albeit objects that are, from the ethnomethodological point of view, observable and reportable within the context of members' ongoing practices. For the ethnomethodologist such claims must have originated "behind members' backs" and, hence, apart from these practices. For the "positivist" they are discarded as matters of entirely private speculation, the assumption being that, in the absence of tangible documentation and some form of measurement, verification of claims about experience within the sphere of public knowledge is now impossible. It is in either case the prejudice of determinate being that rules out the chance to explicate social life in terms of the qualitative immediacy of experience.

2. The flexibility of mind lying behind such inventiveness requires elimination of what Clifford Geertz calls "a confusion, endemic in the West since Plato at least, of the imagined with the imaginary, the fictional with the false, making things out with making them up. The strange idea that reality has an idiom in which it prefers to be described, that its very nature demands we talk about it without fuss—a spade is a spade, a rose is a rose—on pain of illusion, trumpery, and self-bewitchment, leads on to the even stranger idea that, if literalism is lost, so is fact" (Geertz, 1988: 140).

3. The prejudice of determinate being compromises Winch's own effort to do so. Winch posits "rules"—or what he also refers to as "normative standards," or guiding "principles," as the governing criteria of practical understanding. He then recognizes a problem: How are the paralinguistic gestures and vocalizations (e.g., accentuations, intonation shifts) that clearly achieve some form of interactional sensibility to be explained? His solution is to analyze them as "analogous to discursive action," which is to hypostatize to

various aspects of expression a logical apparatus that is, in reality, exterior to their performance and perception. Winch writes: "Even where it would be unnatural to say that a given kind of social relation expresses any ideas of a discursive nature, still it is closer to that general category than it is to that of the interaction of physical forces" (Winch, 1958: 129).

Winch begins with the presupposition that human expression exists originally as a composite of empirical objects. That is to say, the reducibility of expression to its demonstrable features is taken to be intrinsic to the structure of expression prior to reflection. With such a presupposition Winch must overlay a logical model of reflective thought onto these features, for he otherwise has no means of accounting for the intelligibility of behavior. Winch subsumes both the "accepted standards of reasonable behavior current in society" and the subject's "embodiment" of principles of meaningful action under the concept of "rule". He misses the implications of his insight into what he refers to as the "unreflected" character of practical understanding, thereby failing to see that the social context of practical sensibility exists at a level phenomenologically prior to the "acceptance" of an external "standard" or the invocation of an internalized "principle." In short, Winch fails to develop a theory of the embodied capacity for and motivation of meaningful behavior that is commensurate with his own notion of *Verstehen* as an "unreflected sensitivity" to the nonreflective practical understanding being studied. He conceives of meaning in terms of socially bound formulas of rule-following, although it is recognized, paradoxically, that rules of practice are rarely formulated (Winch, 1958: 58). The paradox can be solved only by ridding reflection of the presuppositions that necessitate the formation of the categories that create the paradox, and by rendering philosophical reflection more attuned to the level at which meaning is had in experience prior to being known.

4. Paul Ricoeur writes: "It is the task of an interpretive sociology to ground...'objectivity' [offered to empirical investigation] in the preobjective layer of intersubjective experience *and* to show how the autonomy of the objects with which sociology deals proceeds from this preobjective sphere" (Ricoeur, 1977, 158).

REFERENCES

Agee, J. and Evans, W. 1960. *Let Us Now Praise Famous Men*. New York: Ballantine.

Apple, M. 1979. *Ideology and Curriculum*. London, Boston: Routledge & Kegan Paul.

Arendt, H. 1971. *The Life of the Mind*. New York, London: Harcourt Brace Jovanovich.

Balázs, B. 1979. The Face of Man. In Mast, G. and Cohen, M. (eds.). *Film Theory and Criticism*. 290-298. New York, Oxford: Oxford University Press.

Berger, P. and Luckmann, T. 1966. *The Social Construction of Reality: A Treatise in the Sociology of Knowledge*. New York: Doubleday.

Berman, M. February 27, 1972. Weird but Brilliant Light on the Way We Live. *New York Times Book Review*. 1-10.

Bernstein, B. 1977. *Class, Codes, and Control (Vol. 3): Toward a Theory of Educational Transmission*. London, Boston: Routledge & Kegan Paul.

Bourdieu, P. and J.C. Passeron. 1977. *Reproduction: In Education, Society, & Culture*. Trans. by R. Nice. London, Beverly Hills: Sage.

Bourdieu, P. 1977. *Outline of a Theory of Practice*. Trans. by R. Nice. Cambridge: Cambridge University Press.

—— 1979. *Le Sens Pratique*. Paris: Editions de Minuit.

—— 1981. Men and Machines. In Knorr-Cetina, A. and Cicourel, A.V. (eds.). *Advances in Social Theory and Methodology: Toward an Integration of Micro- and Macro-Sociologies*. 304-317. London, Boston: Routledge & Kegan Paul.

———— 1983. Erving Goffman, Discoverer of the Infinitely Small. *Theory, Culture, and Society* 2 (No. 1): 112-113.

———— 1984. *Distinction: A Social Critique of the Judgment of Taste.* Trans. by R. Nice. Cambridge, Massachusetts: Harvard University Press.

Brett, N. 1981. Human Habits. *Canadian Journal of Philosophy* XI (No. 3): 357-376.

Camic, C. 1986. The Matter of Habit. American Journal of Sociology 91 (No. 5): 1039-1087.

Carnoy, R. 1975. *Schooling in a Corporate Society,* 2nd ed. New York: David McKay Co.

Carrington, P. 1979. Schutz on Transcendental Intersubjectivity in Husserl. *Human Studies* 2 (No. 2): 95-110.

Comte, A. 1974. Fundamental Characteristics of the Positive Method in the Study of Social Phenomena. In Andreski, S. (ed.). *The Essential Comte.* Trans. by M. Clarke. 137-198. London: Croom Helm.

Cooley, C.H. 1908. A Study of the Early Use of Self-Words by a Child. *The Psychological Review* XV (No. 6): 339-357.

———— 1922. *Human Nature and the Social Order.* New York: Charles Scribners & Sons.

Coulter, J. 1989. Cognitive 'Penetrability' and the Emotions. In Franks, D. and McCarthy, E.D. (eds.). *The Sociology of Emotion.* 33-50. New York: JAI Press.

Denzin, N. 1970. Symbolic Interactionism and Ethnomethodology. In Douglas, J. (ed.). *Understanding Everyday Life.* 259-284. Chicago: Aldine Publishing Co.

Dewey, J. 1916. *Democracy and Education.* New York: Free Press.

———— 1922. *Human Nature and Conduct.* New York: Modern Library.

———— 1925. *Experience and Nature,* 1st Edition. Chicago: Open Court.

—— 1929. *Experience and Nature*, 2nd Edition. Chicago: Open Court.

—— 1931. *Philosophy and Civilization*. New York: Capricorn Books.

—— 1958. *Art as Experience*. New York: Capricorn, G.P. Putnam's Sons.

Dilthey, W. 1958. *Gesammelte Schriften*, Vol. VII. Stuttgart: B.G. Teubner.

Dufrenne, M. 1973. *The Phenomenology of Aesthetic Experience*. Trans. by E. Casey, E., et. al. Evanston: Northwestern University Press.

Durkheim, E. 1938. *The Rules of Sociological Method*. Catlin, G. (ed.). Trans. by S. Solovay and J. Mueller. New York: Free Press.

—— 1947. *The Elementary Forms of the Religious Life*. Trans. by S.W. Swain. New York: The Free Press.

Findlay, J. 1963. Some Reflections on Meaning. In Findlay, J. *Language, Mind and Value*. 208-216. London: G. Allen & Unwin.

Garfinkel, H. 1967. *Studies in Ethnomethodology*. New Jersey: Prentice Hall.

Geertz, C. 1973. *The Interpretation of Cultures*. New York: Basic Books.

—— 1988. *Works and Lives: The Anthropologist as Author*. Stanford, California: Stanford University Press.

Gendlin, E. 1965. Expressive Meanings. In Edie, J. (ed.). *An Invitation to Phenomenology*. 240-251. Chicago: Quadrangle Books.

—— 1973. What are the Grounds of Explication? *The Human Context* V (No. 3): 490-511.

Giddens, A. 1979. *Central Problems in Social Theory*. Berkley, Los Angeles: University of California Press.

———— 1981. Agency, Institution, and Time-Space Analysis. In Knorr-Cetina, K. and Cicourel, A.V. (eds.). *Advances in Social Theory and Methodology: Toward an Integration of Micro- and Macro-Sociologies.* 161-174. Boston: Routledge & Kegan Paul.

Gillan, G. 1973. In the Folds of the Flesh. In Gillan, G. (ed.). *The Horizons of the Flesh: Critical Perspectives on the Thought of Merleau-Ponty.* 1-60. Carbondale: Southern Illinois University Press.

Gintis, H. and Bowles, S. 1976. *Schooling in Capitalist America.* New York: Basic Books.

Goffman, E. 1959. *The Presentation of Self in Everyday Life.* New York: Anchor Books.

———— 1961a. *Encounters.* Indianapolis: Bobbs-Merrill.

———— 1961b. *Asylums.* New York: Anchor.

———— 1971. *Relations in Public.* New York: Basic Books.

———— 1974. *Frame Analysis.* New York: Harper and Row.

———— 1981a. *Forms of Talk.* Philadelphia: University of Pennsylvania.

———— 1981b. Reply to Denzin and Keller. *Contemporary Sociology* 10 (No. 1): 60-68.

Goodman, P. 1971. *Speaking and Language.* New York: Random House.

Grene, M. 1959. *Introduction to Existentialism.* Chicago: University of Chicago Press.

Hayim, G.J. 1980. *The Existential Sociology of Jean-Paul Sartre.* Amherst: University of Massachusetts Press.

Heeren, J. 1970. Alfred Schutz and the Sociology of Common-Sense Knowledge. In Douglas, J. (ed.). *Understanding Everyday Life.* 45-56. Chicago: Aldine.

Heidegger, M. 1962. *Being and Time.* Trans. by J. Macquarri and E. Robinson. New York: Harper & Row.

Henry, J. 1963. *Culture Against Man.* New York: Vintage Books.

Heritage, J. 1984. *Garfinkel and Ethnomethodology.* Cambridge: Polity Press.

Husserl, E. 1931. *Ideas: General Introduction to Pure Phenomenology.* Trans. by B. Gibson. New York: Collier-Macmillan.

———— 1960. *Cartesian Meditations: An Introduction to Phenomenology.* Trans. by D. Cairns. The Hague: Nijhoff.

———— 1969. *Formal and Transcendental Logic.* Trans. by D. Cairns. The Hague: Nijhoff.

———— 1970. *The Crisis of European Science and Transcendental Phenomenology.* Trans. by D. Carr, Evanston: Northwestern University Press.

———— 1973. *Experience and Judgment: Investigations in a Genealogy of Logic.* Revised by Landgrebe, L. (ed.). Trans. by J. Churchill and K. Ameriks. Evanston: Northwestern University Press.

Ihde, D. 1973. Singing the World: Language and Perception. In Gillan, G. (ed.). *The Horizons of the Flesh: Critical Perspectives on the Thought of Merleau-Ponty.* 61-77. Carbondale: Southern Illinois University Press.

James, W. 1890. *Principles of Psychology.* New York: Holt.

Karabel, J. and Halsey, A.H. (eds.). 1977. *Power and Ideology in Education.* New York: Oxford University Press.

Kestenbaum, V. 1977. *The Phenomenological Sense of John Dewey: Habit and Meaning.* Atlantic Highlands, New Jersey: Humanities Press.

Kohák, E. 1978. *Idea and Experience: Edmund Husserl's Project of Phenomenology in IDEAS I.* Chicago: University of Chicago Press.

———— 1984. *The Embers and the Stars: A Philosophical Inquiry into the Moral Sense of Nature.* Chicago: University of Chicago Press.

Kosík, K. 1976. *Dialectics of the Concrete: A Study on Problems of*

Man and World. Trans. by K. Kovanda with J Schmidt. Dordecht, Holland: D. Reidel Publishing Co.

Luckmann, T. 1983a. *Life-World and Social Realities*. London: Heinemann.

––––– 1983b. Remarks on Personal Identity: Inner, Social and Historical Time. In Jacobson-Widding, A. (ed.). *Identity: Personal and Socio-Cultural*. 67-91. Uppsala, Sweden: Acta Universitatis Upsaliensis [Uppsala Studies in Cultural Anthropology 5].

Madison, G. 1981. *The Phenomenology of Merleau-Ponty*. Trans. by author. Athens, Ohio: Ohio University Press.

Malamud, B. 1966. *The Fixer*. Harmondsworth, Middlesex, England: Penguin Books.

Mallin, S. 1979. *Merleau-Ponty's Philosophy*. New Haven, London: Yale University Press.

Mannheim, K. 1936. *Ideology and Utopia*. Trans. by L. Wirth and E. Shils. New York: Harvest Books.

Manning, P. 1980. Goffman's Framing Order: Style as Structure. In Ditton, J. (ed.). *The View from Goffman*. 252-284. London: Macmillan.

Marx, K. 1947. Theses on Feuerbach (Appendix). In Marx, K. and Engels, F. *The German Ideology: Parts I & III*. Pascal, P. (ed.). 197-199. New York: International Publishers.

Marx, K. and Engels, F. 1955. *The Communist Manifesto*. Beer, S. (ed.). New York: Appleton-Century Crofts.

Mauss, M. 1979. *Sociology and Psychology*. Trans. by B. Brewster. London: Routledge & Kegan Paul.

Mead, G.H. 1932. *Philosophy of the Present*. Murphy, A. (ed.). Chicago: University of Chicago.

––––– 1934. *Mind, Self, & Society*. Morris, C.W. (ed.). Chicago: University of Chicago.

Merleau-Ponty, M. 1962. *Phenomenology of Perception*. Trans. by C. Smith. Atlantic Highlands, New Jersey: Humanities Press.

—— 1963. *The Structure of Behavior.* Trans. by A. Fisher. Boston: Beacon Press.

—— 1964a. *The Primacy of Perception.* Edie, J. (ed.). Evanston: Northwestern University Press.

—— 1964b. *Signs.* Trans. by R. McCleary. Evanston: Northwestern University Press.

—— 1964c. *Sense and Nonsense.* Trans. by H. Dreyfus and P.A. Dreyfus. Evanston: Northwestern University Press.

—— 1968. *The Visible and the Invisible.* Lefort, C. (ed.). Trans. by A. Lingis. Evanston: Northwestern University.

—— 1970. *Themes from the Lectures.* Trans. by J. O'Neill. Evanston: Northwestern University Press.

—— 1973a. *Consciousness and the Acquisition of Language.* Trans. by H. Silverman. Evanston: Northwestern University Press.

—— 1973b. *The Prose of the World.* Lefort, C. (ed.). Trans. by J. O'Neill. Evanston: Northwestern University Press.

Merton, R. 1957. *Social Theory and Social Structure.* New York: Free Press.

Nisbet, R. 1976. *Sociology as an Art Form.* New York: Oxford University Press.

O'Neill, J. 1970. *Perception, Expression, and History: The Social Phenomenology of Maurice Merleau-Ponty.* Evanston: Northwestern University Press.

Ostrow, J. 1981. Culture as a Fundamental Dimension of Experience: A Discussion of Pierre Bourdieu's Theory of Human Habitus. *Human Studies* 4 (3): 279-297.

—— 1987. Habit and Inhabitance: A Study of Experience in the Classroom. *Human Studies* 10 (2): 213-224.

Owens, T. 1970. *Phenomenology and Intersubjectivity.* The Hague: Nijhoff.

Palmer, R. 1969. *Hermeneutics.* Evanston: Northwestern University Press.

Parsons, A.S. 1973. Constitutive Phenomenology: Schutz's Theory of the We-relation. *Journal of Phenomenological Philosophy* 4 (1): 331-361.

Perls, F.S.; Hefferline, R.F.; Goodman, P. 1951. *Gestalt Therapy.* New York: Julian Press.

Psathas, G. 1977. Goffman's Image of Man. *Humanity & Society* 1 (1): 84-94.

———— 1980. Approaches to the Study of the World in Everyday Life. *Human Studies* 3 (1): 3-17.

Richter, H. 1970. *Virginia Woolf: The Inward Voyage.* Princeton, New Jersey: Princeton University Press.

Ricks, C. 1981. Phew! Oops! Oof! (Review of Erving Goffman's *Forms of Talk. New York Review of Books* XXVIII (12): 42-44.

Ricouer, P. 1966. *Freedom and Nature: The Voluntary and the Involuntary.* Trans. by E. Kohák. Evanston: Northwestern University Press.

———— 1977. Phenomenology and the Social Sciences. In Korenbaum, M. (ed.). *The Annals of Phenomenological Sociology, Vol. II, 1977.* 145-159. Dayton, Ohio: Wright University, 1977.

Sartre, J.P. 1956. *Being and Nothingness.* Trans. by H. Barnes. New York: Washington Square Press.

———— 1967. Consciousness of Self and Knowledge of Self. In Lawrence, N. and O'Connor, D. (eds.). *Readings in Existential Phenomenology.* 113-142. Englewood Cliffs, New Jersey: Prentice-Hall, Inc.

Scheler, M. 1954. *The Nature of Sympathy.* Trans. by P. Heath. New Haven, Connecticut: Yale University Press.

Schmidt, J. 1985. *Maurice Merleau-Ponty: Between Phenomenology and Structuralism.* New York: St. Martins.

Schutz, A. 1932. *Der sinnhafte Aufbau der sozialen Welt.* Unpublished translation of selected passages by K.H. Wolff. Vienna: Julius Springer.

—— 1962a. Common Sense and Scientific Interpretation of Human Action. Schutz, A. *Collected Papers, Vol. I: The Problem of Social Reality.* Natanson, M. (ed.). 3-47. The Hague: Nijhoff.

—— 1962b. Phenomenology and the Social Sciences. In Schutz, A. *Collected Papers, Vol. I: The Problem of Social Reality.* Natanson, M. (ed.). 118-139. The Hague: Nijhoff.

—— 1962c. Husserl's Importance for the Social Sciences. In Schutz, A. *Collected Papers, Vol. I: The Problem of Social Reality.* Natanson, M. (ed.). 140-149. The Hague: Nijhoff.

—— 1962d. Sartre's Theory of the Alter Ego. In Schutz, A. *Collected Papers, Vol. I: The Problem of Social Reality.* Natanson, M. (ed.). 181-199. The Hague: Nijhoff.

—— 1964a. The Stranger: An Essay in Social Psychology. In Schutz, A. *Collected Papers, Vol. II: Studies in Social Theory.* Brodersen, A. (ed.). 91-105. The Hague: Nijhoff.

—— 1964b. Making Music Together: A Study in Social Relationship. In Schutz, A. *Collected Papers, Vol. II: Studies in Social Theory.* 159-178. Broderson, A. (ed.). The Hague: Nijhoff.

—— 1966a. Edmund Husserl's *Ideas: Vol. II.* In Schutz, A. *Collected Papers, Vol. III: Studies in Phenomenological Philosophy.* Schutz, I. (ed.). 15-39. The Hague: Nijhoff.

—— 1966b. The Problem of Transcendental Intersubjectivity in Husserl. In Schutz, A. *Collected Papers, Vol. III: Studies in Phenomenological Philosophy.* Schutz, I. (ed.). 51-84. The Hague: Nijhoff.

—— 1967. *The Phenomenology of the Social World.* Trans. by G. Walsh and F. Lehnert. Evanston: Northwestern University Press.

—— 1970. *Reflections on the Problem of Relevance.* Zaner, R. (ed.). New Haven, London: Yale University Press.

Schutz, A. & Luckmann, T. 1974. *The Structures of the Life-World.* London: Heinemann.

Schwartz, P. & Lever, J. 1976. Fear and Loathing at a College Mixer. *Urban Life* 4 (4): 413-430.

Sharrock, W. & Anderson, B. 1986. *The Ethnomethodologists.* Chichester, London, New York: Ellis Howard Limited & Tavistock.

Sheridan, J. 1973. *Once More—From the Middle: A Philosophical Anthropology.* Athens, Ohio: Ohio University Press.

Simmel, G. 1950. Sociability. In Wolff, K.H. (ed. and trans.). *The Sociology of George Simmel.* 40-57. New York: The Free Press.

——— 1959. The Aesthetic Significance of the Face. Trans. by L. Ferguson. In Wolff, K.H. (ed.), *Georg Simmel, 1858-1918.* 276-281. Columbus, OH: Ohio State University Press.

Spring, J. 1972. *Education and the Rise of the Corporate State.* Boston: Beacon Press.

——— 1976. *The Sorting Machine.* New York: David McKay Co.

Stevens, R. 1974. *James and Husserl: The Foundations of Meaning.* The Hague: Nijhoff.

Sudnow, D. 1979. *Talk's Body: A Meditation Between Two Keyboards.* New York: Alfred A. Knopf.

Thomas, W.I. 1923. *The Unadjusted Girl.* New York: Little Brown & Low.

Truzzi, M. (ed.). *Verstehen: Subjective Understanding in the Social Sciences.* Reading, Massachusetts: Addison-Wesley.

Webb, R. 1976. *The Presence of the Past: John Dewey and Alfred Schutz on the Genesis and Organization of Experience.* Gainesville, Florida: University Presses of Florida.

Weber, M. 1947. *The Theory of Social and Economic Organization.* Parsons, T. (ed.). Trans. by A. Henderson and T. Parsons. New York: Oxford University Press.

———— 1949. *The Methodology of the Social Sciences.* Shils, A. and Finch, H. (eds. & trans.). New York: Free Press.

Wilshire, B. 1982. *Role Theory and Identity.* Bloomington: Indiana University Press.

Winch, P. 1958. *The Idea of a Social Science.* London: Routledge & Kegan Paul.

Wolff, K.H. 1976. *Surrender and Catch: Experience and Inquiry Today.* Dordrecht-Holland, Boston: D. Reidel.

———— 1982. Into Alfred Schutz's World. Presented at the Meeting of the World Institute for Phenomenological Research at the 79th Annual Meeting of the American Philosophy Association (Eastern Division), Baltimore, December 29.

———— 1984. Surrender-and-Catch and Phenomenology. *Human Studies* 7 (2): 191-210.

Woolf, V. 1927. *To the Lighthouse.* New York: Modern library.

INDEX

Agee, J., 21, 62-66
Anderson, B., 95n.5, 97-98n.1
Arendt, H., 87
Augustine, S., 105n.7

Balázs, B., 45, 86-87
Berger, P., 7, 21-22, 34, 97-98n.1
Bergson, H., 38, 105n.7
Body: as preobjective, 12-13, 27-28,
   40-41, 60, 80; as object, 12, 40-43;
   as sign-signitive system, 12, 39,
   41, 46, 104-5n.6
Bourdieu, P.: on determinism, 70,
   73-74, 79; theory of habitus,
   16-18, 68-73, 96n.6, 115-16n.4;
   on intellectualism, 59; on
   phenomenology, 17, 68-69, 73;
   on occasionalist illusion, 9;
   concept of tempo, 76, 117-18n.9
Brett, N., 10

Camic, C., 10-11, 95-97n.6
Comte, A., 4-5
Consciousness, intentionality of,
   12, 22-23, 30; as corporeal, 40-43;
   as obviated by habitus, 73;
   operative and thetic, 8, 30;
   preobjective foundation of, 28,
   43, 69, 90. See also Sensitivity, as
   social foundation of
   consciousness
Contact, experiential, 13, 98n.4.

See also Intersubjectivity, as
   preobjective contact; Situation,
   preobjective structure of
Cooley, C.H., 14, 51-54, 61,
   109nn.1, 2, 110n.4
Coulter, J., 108n.15

Denzin, N., 109-110n.3
Descartes, R., 41
Dewey, J.: on denotative method of
   philosophy, 2, 79, 85; on dualism
   of subject and world, 3-4, 47,
   106n.10; concept of expression,
   46, 49; theory of habit, 10-11, 18,
   30-31, 34, 44, 85-86, 89-90, 97n.6,
   99-100n.10, 100-101n.13,
   101-102n.16; on qualitative
   immediacy of experience, 1-3, 54,
   99n.8; on sense and signification,
   2-3, 7, 11, 41
Dilthey, W., 5, 93nn.1, 2
Dufrenne, M., 32
Durkheim, E., 4-5, 51, 88, 93-94n.3,
   96n.6

Empirical evidence, 5, 61, 86, 88,
   118-19n.1
Ethnomethodology, 7, 95n.5,
   97-98n.1, 113-114n.13, 114n.14,
   115n.1, 118-119n.1
Experience: concept of, 3, 93n.1;
   description of, 47, 86-89, 119n.2;